Critical Thinking
for Students

Visit our How To website at www.howto.co.uk

At www.howto.co.uk you can engage in conversation with our authors – all of whom have 'been there and done that' in their specialist fields. You can get access to special offers and additional content but most importantly you will be able to engage with, and become a part of, a wide and growing community of people just like yourself.

At www.howto.co.uk you'll be able to talk and share tips with people who have similar interests and are facing similar challenges in their lives. People who, just like you, have the desire to change their lives for the better – be it through moving to a new country, starting a new business, growing their own vegetables, or writing a novel.

At www.howto.co.uk you'll find the support and encouragement you need to help make your aspirations a reality.

You can go direct to www.critical-thinking-for-students.co.uk which is part of the main How To site.

How To Books strives to present authentic, inspiring, practical information in their books. Now, when you buy a title from **How To Books,** you get even more than just words on a page.

Critical Thinking for Students

Learn the skills of analysing, evaluating and producing arguments

Thoroughly revised
and updated
FOURTH
EDITION

Roy van den Brink-Budgen

howtobooks

Published by How To Books Ltd
Spring Hill House, Spring Hill Road,
Begbroke, Oxford OX5 1RX
Tel: (01865) 375794 Fax: (01865) 379162
info@howtobooks.co.uk
www.howtobooks.co.uk

How To Books greatly reduce the carbon footprint of their books by sourcing their
typesetting and printing in the UK.

First edition 1996
Second edition 1999
Third edition 2003
Reprinted 2001, 2002, 2003 (twice), 2004 (three times), 2005 (twice), 2007, 2009
Fourth edition 2010
Reprinted 2010
Reprinted 2011

British Library Cataloguing in Publication Data.
A catalogue record for this book is available from the British Library.

ISBN 978 1 84528 386 5

Cover design by Baseline Arts Ltd, Oxford
Produced for How To Books by Deer Park Productions, Tavistock
Typeset by PDQ Typesetting, Newcastle-under-Lyme, Staffordshire
Printed and bound by Bell & Bain Ltd, Glasgow

NOTE: The material contained in this book is set out in good faith for general guidance
and no liability can be accepted for loss or expense incurred as a result of relying in
particular circumstances on statements made in the book. The laws and regulations are
complex and liable to change, and readers should check the current position with the
relevant authorities before making personal arrangements.

CONTENTS

PREFACE TO THE FOURTH EDITION

The first edition of this book was published as long ago as 1996. At the time, it broke new ground in trying to bring the subject to a wide audience. Fortunately it (and subsequent editions) sold in encouragingly large numbers, justifying my belief that the subject of Critical Thinking should be available beyond the universities.

There are now quite a few textbooks around on Critical Thinking. They come in many versions. Some scream at you in vibrant colour and shout 'key point' whenever particular words are used. Some shout less but take you down somewhat unimaginative routes, noting weighty things, but without stopping to see how the subject works in the world around us. Both types fail to show what a wonderfully creative subject this is.

Critical Thinking is an exciting subject because it will change your thinking by showing you all sorts of possibilities, all sorts of ways of looking at things. It will encourage you to ask lots of questions. What does this mean? What more do I need to know? What's the problem with what that person has said? You don't need someone to bellow 'key point' at you, when you're asking and answering questions like these. You'll just experience the fizz of it all when you do.

This book continues in the tradition of its earlier editions. Though it's been completely rewritten, the promise of the book is the same. If you read this book, you'll be much more skilful in how you think. Much more. You'll have thoughts about such things as these, as well as other significant things.

> Half of the world's population has seen at least one James Bond film.
> In Britain, trousers cause twice as many accidents as are caused by chainsaws.
> None of the world's richest 100 men is married to a redhead.

Over to you. . .

Roy van den Brink-Budgen

To Annie, *sine qua non*

GIVING CLAIMS A SIGNIFICANCE

WHAT IS CRITICAL THINKING?

It might seem odd to have to start a book on a subject by having to ask the question of what it's about. In the case of Critical Thinking, however, it's a question that we need to ask. It's not that clear what it is about. Just saying the words doesn't seem to get us very far: 'critical' (in what way?); 'thinking' (about what?). We can look at various definitions and they still won't make it particularly clear what's going on. They won't tell you quickly what it is, so that you'll be able to say 'Ah! I begin to see it now. I can see what it's about.' However, once you've read the first few pages of this book, you'll be saying something very close to that.

It's often said that Critical Thinking is all about the study of arguments. So you'll find some people (teachers of the subject, and others) fretting right at the start of proceedings about the difference between arguments in Critical Thinking and other sorts of arguments. (I once fretted like them, but have long since seen the light.) Saying that Critical Thinking is all about arguments is something like saying that music is all about a series of notes. It doesn't capture very much about what's going on when we do Critical Thinking or why it's so important. So we're not even going to look at or ask about arguments at this stage. Walk away from anyone who still insists on focusing on the question 'What's the difference between a Critical Thinking argument and other arguments?' at the beginning, and tell them that you're off to look at far more significant things.

Critical Thinking is much better seen as the activity of looking at the possible meaning and significance of claims. However, I can see that this also doesn't convey that much. What's a 'claim'?

CLAIMS

I use the term in a very simple way. When somebody says 'such-and-such is the case' then they're making a claim. Here are some examples:

> The weather is much less good than was predicted.

> This supermarket's products are much cheaper than that one's.

> Fish can feel pain.

> The number of people surviving into very old age is increasing at a fast rate.

> Teachers get longer holidays than anyone else.

> Singapore is one of the healthiest countries in the world.

Critical Thinking takes claims like these and asks questions about them. This can include the question 'Is it true?' but normally Critical Thinking would ask questions like 'Is this claim telling us something significant?' and 'What else do we need to know in order to respond to this claim?'

In a way, claims on their own normally don't tell us anything beyond the obvious point that's being claimed. The claim (piece of information, or whatever it is) just sits there. It's up to us to do something with it. It's a bit like how a painting just hangs there. It does nothing until someone looks at it and says, 'That's good/beautiful/weird/bad/meaningless/expensive...' So, in a similar way, when you come along and respond to the claim, 'This is surprising (because)...', then you've started to give the claim significance or meaning. You've given it a life beyond the words, if you like.

We'll now look in some detail at what we can do with a claim. We'll look at an example.

> Including President Obama, five out of the most recent seven US presidents have been left-handed.

We said above that Critical Thinking should be seen as the activity of looking at the possible meaning and significance of claims. So what is the possible significance of this claim? Is there any way that we're looking at anything significant here? At the very least, the claim will probably have surprised you. And the fact that it has surprised you is a big hint that there might be some significance to be found.

Is it telling us anything more significant than the next claim?

All US presidents have been men.

The claim that all US presidents have been men is, in an important way, telling us something beyond a simple piece of information. But what it's telling us will vary from reader to reader. What is its significance? Of course, though we might predict that there will be a female president of the US before 2020, we would probably find it relatively easy to explain why there hasn't been one so far. (Though there have been other countries which have had a female political leader – Margaret Thatcher is an obvious example – the US is not at all unusual in not having had one.) We could say that this claim is significant because it tells us something about the dominance of men in US politics. The claim shows a pattern that has at least one straightforward meaning.

What about the next claim?

Four US presidents have been assassinated.

This claim is one that might or might not be significant. On its own, it's difficult to say. To know if it's got a significance, we need more information. What else do we need to know? The next two questions are particularly important.

- How many US presidents have there been?

- How many other leaders have been assassinated?

Answers to these questions will help us to answer the next one.

- Quite simply, is four a significant number? (Is it low or high – how many would we have expected?)

By now, you can hopefully see already that, in looking to see if a claim is significant, we very often need to ask questions about it. These questions might help us to answer the central questions 'What does this mean?' and 'Is this significant?'

Let's return to our first claim and start to ask questions about it to try to establish any significance.

Including President Obama, five out of the most recent seven US presidents have been left-handed.

Here are some questions we could (or perhaps should) ask:

- What proportion of the US population is left-handed?

- What about the presidents before the last seven?

- If Barack Obama had lost the election in 2008, would that have meant that four of the most recent seven US presidents had been left-handed?

- How many other countries have (had) left-handed leaders?

You can see that, to give a claim a significance, to decide what it might mean, we often need to know more about it. By this we mean that we often need to know more about other things that are relevant to it. We'll look at the first three of these questions to illustrate this.

- What proportion of the US population is left-handed?

The proportion is about 10 per cent (the same as in other countries). So, we should expect that, all things being equal, a US President is much less likely to be left-handed than right-handed. As a result, the evidence on the very high proportion of left-handers in the last seven presidents takes on a possible significance. One calculation is that there is only a 1 in 1000 chance of there being five out of seven left-handed presidents if all things were equal. (Of course, we have to accept that 1 in 1000 chances do occur, so we have to accept that it might be just an interesting coincidence that so many presidents are left-handed.)

- If Barack Obama had lost the election in 2008, would that have meant that four of the most recent seven US presidents had been left-handed?

Interestingly, no. His Republican opponent was John McCain, also left-handed! If we look further back, the right-handed George W. Bush won the presidential election of 2000 by beating Al Gore in a highly disputed result. The result was very close and, some argue, should have been given the other way. If that had been the case, then Al Gore would have won. And, if he had, that would have been another left-hander on the list!

A further question was this one.

● What about the US presidents before the most recent seven?

Well, interestingly, only 3 out of the previous 36 were left-handed. This is about what we would expect from our earlier piece of evidence on left-handers making up about 10 per cent of the US population. So what is it about recent presidents that is different?

You can see that, before we can do anything with the piece of evidence on the high proportion of recent US presidents being left-handed, we needed to ask and answer questions about its possible meaning. We've done that and we're probably now considering that the evidence does appear to have a significance.

This would take us in two related directions. One would be to look at possible explanations (why is this the case?). The other would be to look at what *follows* from the evidence and the explanation. (In looking at what follows from a claim, we're into what are called 'inferences'.) We'll be looking at the subject of explanation in detail in the next chapter (when we'll return to looking at the evidence on left-handed presidents), and at inferences throughout the rest of the book.

Earlier, we said that Critical Thinking should be seen as 'the activity of looking at the possible meaning and significance of claims'. We then looked at a claim, which was a piece of evidence. We need to return to this point. By claims, you'll remember, we mean when it is said that 'such-and-such is the case'. The 'such-and-such' that we're referring to can be not only evidence but also predictions, recommendations, and principles.

We'll now have a look at some further examples of claims of evidence (or what we'll call evidence-claims).

EVIDENCE-CLAIMS

Evidence-claims include statistical evidence, scientific evidence, historical evidence, and evidence that 'so-and-so said something'.

We've had a look at some statistical evidence on US presidents. Here are some other statistical evidence-claims:

In the United Arab Emirates (UAE) there are 210 males for every 100 females.

The life expectancy of professional cyclists is about 50.

As with our evidence-claims on US presidents, we would need to ask questions about these claims in order to look at what significance there might be with each of these. (What is the ratio of males to females in other countries? What is the normal life expectancy in the countries that have professional cyclists? What is the normal life expectancy of professional sportspeople?) As you can see, each of the claims will raise further questions about explanation (Why are there so many males compared to females in the UAE?) and also inference ('So don't become a professional cyclist if you want a long life.').

Here's a claim which is scientific evidence:

Using foul language after hitting your thumb with a hammer can increase tolerance of pain.

In this example, we're very interested in looking for possible explanations for the evidence. But, as with statistical evidence, we'd also want to ask questions about the significance of the evidence. One question is obviously, 'How foul does the foul language have to be to work?' Another one would be, 'What if someone uses really foul language lots of the time anyway? Would it work for them?' Questions like this could then be linked to possible explanations to lead towards a possible inference ('So next time you hit your thumb with a hammer, just shout ****.').

There are plenty of historical evidence-claims. Here's an example:

Between 1791 and 1892, there were 10,300 executions and 900,000 sentences of imprisonment in England and Wales.

To work out the significance of this evidence-claim, we need to ask the same sort of questions as before. This is because, before we ask any questions, its significance remains locked. Are these figures higher or lower than we would have expected (or are they about right)? Do we need to know more? If so, what do we need to know? How might answers to these questions add anything to the possible significance of this historical evidence-claim?

Do these further related evidence-claims add anything?

Between 1791 and 1892, there were 222 different offences that carried the death penalty in England and Wales.

Between 1791 and 1892, 97,000 people in England and Wales were sentenced to transportation.

The first might be relevant in considering the significance of the number of people executed. The second might be relevant in considering the scale of punishment for crime during the nineteenth century. But, of course, we would need to know much more in order to give a full account of the significance of the first claim on executions and imprisonment.

Historical evidence-claims can be reports of what someone said (or is supposed to have said). Dr Thomas Neill Cream was executed in 1892 for poisoning several people. He was one of those suspected at the time of being Jack the Ripper. His final words in the two seconds just before he was hanged were

'I am Jack...'

So what might that unfinished claim mean? That he was Jack the Ripper? That he knew or helped Jack the Ripper ('I am Jack the Ripper's friend/brother/...')? Claims can sometimes take us tantalisingly nowhere.

One of the most notorious examples of the disputed significance of a claim are the words, 'Let him have it, Chris'. These were apparently the words used by a young man named Derek Bentley, already under arrest, to his young friend, Chris Craig, who had a gun. Craig fired his gun and a policeman was shot and died. The big dispute is whether the words meant 'shoot the policeman' or 'let the policeman have the gun'. Unfortunately for the 19-year-old Derek, the jury took it to be the first and he was hanged a few weeks later. The 16-year-old Chris was too young to be executed so is still alive today. You can see a somewhat passionate account of the case at **http://www.bbc.co.uk/dna/h2g2/ A9115229**.

Claims that somebody said something are commonly reported in newspapers, on TV, and on the radio. Here's an example from *The Times* of 3 August 2009.

Ken Stanborough accidentally dropped his daughter's iPod Touch on the floor and, having noticed that it was then getting hotter and that vapour seemed to be coming from it, he threw it outside where 'within 30 seconds there was a pop, a big puff of smoke and it went 10ft in the air'.

We would treat this evidence-claim in the same way as any other. This means that we would ask any relevant questions about it in order to consider whether it had any significance. An obvious one would be, 'Have there been other cases of exploding iPod Touches?' Though the explanation for the exploding iPod is not something that we can necessarily explore (being a technical issue), we could look for possible inferences from the report. For example, 'You should take care if your iPod Touch feels hot.'

We find these evidence-claims wherever we look. As we have seen, on their own they do nothing. They just sit there being stated. It is only when something is done with them that something happens.

PREDICTION-CLAIMS

As well as claims of evidence, we also have predictions that 'such-and-such will happen'. Such prediction-claims are normally based on some existing evidence-claims.

There is a baby already born today that will live until it's 250.

In order to consider the possible significance of this prediction-claim, we would again ask questions. 'Is this a one-off extra-long-living baby or is this baby an example of what will become a general trend?' 'Might a 16-year-old reading these words today still be thinking critically in 2160?' We would need to ask explanation questions (Why is this possible?) before we could make claims of inference (So. . .). Thus the claim, 'So we should scrap all this strange business of paying people pensions before they're 75', might follow from this prediction-claim (but might not).

In an important way, then, we deal with prediction-claims in the same way as we deal with evidence-claims. We ask questions about their significance. What do we need to know to give this prediction a significance? For example, in the one about the long-surviving baby, without doing this, the claim just sits there. We are clearly not meant to see it in the same way as the claim that 'There is a baby born today that will live until it's 85'. It's meant to be significant. It shouts at you to be explained and then for at least one inference to be drawn from it.

RECOMMENDATIONS

What about claims that are recommendations? They also have to be seen in terms of possible significance. Look at the following recommendation.

We should take more exercise.

This again just sits there, without any significance unless and until someone gives it some. It might be that asking for explanations is important (What evidence-claims support the recommendation?). Questions can (and should) be asked about the words used. What is meant by 'more'? More than what? How much is 'more'? What is meant by 'exercise'? Jogging? Going to the gym? Walking? Without having answers to questions like these, the significance of the claim is a problem. And until the significance is clarified, the claim cannot usefully be used to draw an inference ('So you should join a gym.').

PRINCIPLES

A bit like recommendations are claims that are principles. We'll spend some time looking at these in detail in Chapter 8, but we can note at this point that principles are general claims about what ought or ought not to be done.

> Cheating in sport can never be justified.

You can see that this principle is no more than a claim. 'Such-and-such is the case' fits a principle exactly. It might be thought, however, that we don't need to fret as much about significance. Perhaps, it might be argued, we don't need to ask as many questions about principle-claims.

However, principle-claims are loaded with problems of significance. As with the recommendation about exercise, we need to ask lots of questions about the meaning of words. What is meant by 'cheating'? Is it 'breaking the rules'? What is meant by 'sport'? Is poker-playing a sport? Is 'eating as many burgers as you can in a minute'? What is meant by 'never'? What about the problem of losing in football when you played for the national team in Saddam Hussein's Iraq (when losing would probably result in you and your family being shot by one of Saddam's sons)?

We can see then that principles stand as claims whose significance needs testing by asking questions. Before we can usefully draw inferences from them, we have to ask these questions.

SUMMARY

In this chapter, we have seen that doing Critical Thinking is very much about asking questions – questions about the significance of claims. These questions are very often to do with meaning.

- What *might* that claim mean?

- What *does* that claim mean?

- What does that word/term mean as it is used in this claim?

- Are there any problems with the meaning of words and terms in the claim?

We've so far been looking at claims where nothing has been done with them. We've looked at possible significance to see what *could* be done with them. But, if someone has already done something with a claim, we need to do the same sort of thing in order to assess what meaning they have given it.

- What meaning has been given to that evidence-claim?

- *Should* that meaning have been given?

We'll look at this very big area of Critical Thinking throughout much of the rest of this book. Critical Thinking is indeed all about the significance of claims, very much including what people do with them.

We're now going to spend time on a very important aspect of looking at claims – looking for and at explanations.

2

EXPLANATIONS

If you look at other books on Critical Thinking, you'll find that explanations are consigned to a very minor role in the proceedings. For example, in Stella Cottrell's book *Critical Thinking Skills* we find explanations dismissed in less than half a page out of the book's 250 pages. This is bizarre.

The normal justification for treating explanations as having very little to do with Critical Thinking is that they aren't central the study of 'arguments', which is what Critical Thinking is often seen to be all about. Here we go again. Unfortunately, the emphasis on arguments as the starting and end points of Critical Thinking can cause a lot of problems. Here it ends up obscuring the importance of explanations in the process of looking at the significance of claims. Putting explanations into such a minor position is a failure to understand their importance, and a failure to understand the importance of looking at the significance of claims.

INFERENCES

However, before we turn our attention to the detail of explanations, it would be very useful to be clearer about what we mean by the term 'inference'. You will remember that we used it in Chapter 1, and indicated its meaning by using 'So. . .'. This focuses us well on what's going on when we're making or looking at an inference. When a claim is used to claim something else, then we have inference going on. For example:

Derek Bentley had a mental age of 11, so he should not have been hanged.

In this example, the first claim about Derek Bentley's mental age is used to infer (draw) the second claim that he shouldn't have been hanged. It can be shown like this:

Derek Bentley had a mental age of 11. → He should not have been hanged.

When we've produced a line of inference like this (claim → claim) we've got a basic 'argument', as the term is used in Critical Thinking. Arguments can get much more complex than claim → claim, but only because they can use lots of claims. However, if you just hold on to the idea of claim → claim, then you'll know what we're doing when we're talking about 'arguments'. It's not much more complicated than that, so it's astonishing how many writers and teachers spend so much time claiming it is.

The only other thing to note is that the process of claim → claim is designed to persuade others that this is the case. The person making the inference is saying 'here is a claim, so this follows from it'. We might or might not agree, and then we're straight back where we were in the first chapter, looking at the significance of claims. Does this claim mean what that person says it does? If it doesn't, then claim → claim doesn't (or might not) work.

With little or no pain, we have given ourselves a working guide to inference and thus 'arguments' as used in Critical Thinking. We'll return to looking in more detail at inference and argument in later chapters. But let's get back to what should be of great interest in Critical Thinking – explanations.

EXPLAINING CLAIMS

We saw in the first chapter that when we looked at claims, especially evidence-claims, we were often needing to ask questions about how we could explain the claim. In that chapter, we spent some time looking at the claim about the recent high proportion of left-handed US presidents.

We got so far with looking at the significance of the claim by asking questions to give us more information. But, in order to push further on with considering the significance of the claim, we need to look at possible explanations. Quite simply, unless and until we do, we can't draw any inference from the claim.

> Including President Obama, five out of the most recent seven US presidents have been left-handed. So...? (claim → claim?)

In Chapter 1, we saw that this claim had a possible significance in the light of the evidence that only about 10 per cent of the US population were left-handed. This possible significance very much pushes us to ask the question, 'So how can we explain why so many recent US presidents have been left-handed?'

Here are some possible explanations.

1. Left-handed people think differently. They think intuitively (that is, they understand things without having to think them through). This might be useful for political success.

2. Left-handed people often had to deal with strong pressure from teachers to write with their right hand. Having to learn how to deal with difficulties like this and other aspects of a world dominated by right-handedness could make the left-hander a stronger, more determined person.

3. Because of the way in which their brains are 'wired', some left-handed people process language on both sides of the brain (unlike right-handed people). This could make them really good at making speeches which, in turn, would be useful in being elected as president.

4. Left-handed people tend to be more dominant, more self-centred, more pushy, all qualities that would be relevant for becoming president.

5. Left-handed people often go into specific jobs. For example, we find a relatively high proportion of left-handed lawyers, architects, artists, actors, and engineers. Barack Obama was a lawyer, as were the left-handed Presidents Clinton and Ford. The left-handed President Reagan was an actor. (An earlier left-handed president was Herbert Hoover, an engineer.)

Each of these could be possible explanations, and perhaps together they all add up to *the* explanation. But, as with claims, we need to ask questions of them.

For example, the second one – about left-handers being made to write with their right hand – wouldn't fit Obama very well. This practice was still found in the 1950s and possibly even the early 1960s, but not beyond that, so he is too young (being born in 1961) to have been affected by it. (Interestingly, it might, however, explain why there were far fewer left-handed presidents before the ones that we've been looking at: perhaps they were required to be right-handed.)

The fifth one is interesting because it might provide an explanation which shows that it isn't the left-handedness as such that's the thing we should be looking at. Perhaps we should ask, 'How many recent US presidents have been lawyers?' (Answer = 3 of the most recent 7, or 42.86 per cent.) And what percentage of the US population are lawyers? (Answer = 0.36 per cent) And what percentage of US lawyers are left-handed? (Possibly as much as 40 per cent!)

So here we have a new possible significance for the original claim we looked at. Given that lawyers have a relatively high rate of being elected as president, and given the higher rate of left-handedness in lawyers, we would expect that there will be a relatively high rate of left-handed presidents.

The claim about left-handed US presidents highlights well the importance of explanations in Critical Thinking. Explanations can focus us on the possible significance of claims. By doing this, they help us to look at what might be inferred from claims. (In the US presidents example, you might well have made the point that, in a way, all we've done is to solve one problem by creating another. OK, we're clearer now about why there have been so many left-handed presidents. But why are so many presidents lawyers? Perhaps you can think further about that one.)

We can show the way in which claims, explanations, and inference are connected by using a simple diagram. Starting with an evidence-claim, we can see that our route to an inference lies through explanation. The relationship between evidence and explanation is shown by arrows going both ways, to emphasise that evidence is normally part of explanations, and that explanations often focus us on to what sort of evidence we need to look for.

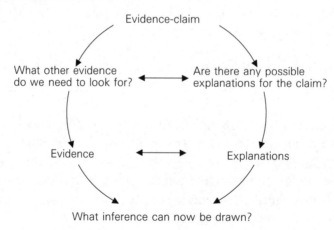

A relatively high rate of recent US presidents have been lawyers + a relatively high rate of US lawyers are left-handed → *it is not surprising that a high rate of US presidents are left-handed.*

You will see that a possible inference has now been drawn (in italics). You could probably think of others. (*There will continue to be a relatively large number of left-handed US presidents.*)

Before you leave this example, you might want to consider whether the other explanations that we gave are significant. But, before you do that, let's just return to a question about the evidence on this subject that we asked in Chapter 1.

How many other countries have (had) left-handed leaders?

The relevance of this question should be clear. If there is a feature of left-handedness that tends to push left-handed people towards the top in politics, should we not find it in countries other than the US too? If we don't find this, then we might have to look for an explanation that fits the US but doesn't have to fit generally.

In the UK, there were only two left-handed Prime Ministers between 1945–2009: Winston Churchill and James Callaghan. That was two out of twelve, and they were in power for only about 12 per cent of the time. However, the present UK Prime Minister (2010), David Cameron, is also left-handed, so this makes three out of thirteen since 1945. In Canada, there's never been a left-handed Prime Minister. In Israel, however, the Prime Minister is the left-handed Benjamin Netanyahu (as at October 2009). You can usefully research this further yourself, but there seems to be no other country with the same recent dominance of left-handed political leaders as the US.

You will remember that lines of inference (or 'arguments') are seen as having the function of persuading the reader/listener that 'because such-and-such is the case, it therefore follows that...' Some see a defining feature of explanations as being the opposite. They say that explanations don't have the function of persuading us of something, but instead merely 'account for' something. However, this works only with some explanations.

Winter is the more common time for outbreaks of flu. This could be for a number of reasons. One is that, in winter, people spend far more time indoors so people can infect others more easily. Another is that, in winter, there is less sunshine, so the ultraviolet rays in sunshine are less likely to kill the flu virus.

In this explanation, the claim that 'Winter is the more common time for outbreaks of flu' is the claim that is being explained. The writer isn't trying to persuade us that this is the case, in that presumably we're not going to dispute it. (We might, of course, dispute the author's explanation, offering other reasons as to why flu is more common in winter. Importantly, we're now right back to the question of the significance of claims.)

However, there are explanations which aren't just accounting for something. Such explanations deal with claims whose significance might be highly disputed. Here's an example. There have been many explanations as to why the *Titanic* sank in 1912. Though few people are going to dispute whether or not the ship sank, there are considerable disputes as to the explanation or explanations. One recent explanation is that of the quality of the rivets used in the building of the ship.

> The *Titanic* sank in 1912 because of the poor quality of the rivets used on the ship. According to two scientists, the shipbuilders Harland and Wolff were having considerable trouble getting enough top quality rivets for the three ships they were building all at the same time – the *Titanic*, the *Olympic*, and the *Britannic*. It was decided therefore to use what were termed 'best' rivets instead of the usual 'best-best'. These poorer-quality rivets were less strong than the 'best-best'. Furthermore, these poorer-quality rivets were used on the bow and the stern of the Titanic, with the stronger ones being used for the centre of the hull, because it was calculated that this was where the ship needed to be the strongest. Unfortunately, it was the bow of the ship that was hit by the iceberg, forcing the poor-quality rivets to fracture.

So what's going on here?

This is an explanation of why the *Titanic* sank after hitting an iceberg. In this sense, it could be said to be accounting for why it sank. But it's importantly doing something different. It amounts to an explanation of why poor-quality rivets would have caused the *Titanic* to be so badly damaged. To see it in terms of responses to a claim, let's break it up into its parts.

> **Claim**: Poor-quality rivets were used in the building of the *Titanic*.

> **Explanation** (also a claim): There was a shortage of high-quality rivets at the time of the building of the *Titanic*.

> **Claim** (+ explanation): The poor-quality rivets were used on the bow of the ship. (The high-quality rivets were used in the centre of the ship because it was calculated that that was where the ship needed to be at its strongest.)

Claim: The *Titanic*'s bow hit an iceberg.

Claim/inference (as a result of explanations): The *Titanic* sank because of the poor quality of the rivets used on the ship.

We can see that the whole thing is a series of claims, with explanations forming a central part of what's going on here. Though few people dispute that the *Titanic* sank after hitting an iceberg, it is not the sinking as such that is the centre of this sequence of claims. It is the explanation for it.

Here we have then an explanation which is very much ripe for Critical Thinking. We could ask questions about the claims being made.

What about the other two ships being built at the same time? Did they also sink?

The *Britannic* hit a mine in 1916 and sank. The *Olympic* carried on for 24 years, sailing until it was 'retired'.

Has evidence from the wreck of the *Titanic* been found to support the weak rivets explanation?

Yes. It was always expected that a large gash in the bow would have been found, caused by the iceberg tearing into the metal. However, this is not the case. There are six narrow slits in the bow where the metal plates have parted, allowing water to rush in.

What other explanations have been given for why the Titanic sank?

There are plenty of these. They include the unusually large number of icebergs in April 1912, the lack of binoculars to see icebergs, and the calmness of the sea (so that there were no waves to be seen breaking on the iceberg). You can look for further explanations. (Indeed, it is very likely that the *Titanic* sank for a number of reasons.)

Interestingly, we have an example here in which a large number of possible explanations can be seen as being part of 'the explanation'. Our previous work on left-handed US presidents is also very likely to fit with this type of explanation. An explanation made up of a series of contributory explanations has implications for any inferences drawn from it. Thus, an inference on the claim about the high proportion of left-handed US presidents will have to be judged against the range of possible explanations for the claim.

We can now see explanations as a way of focusing us on to the significance of evidence-claims. By doing this, they help us to draw useful inferences and to assess inferences that others have drawn.

Where we have (or use) only one explanation for evidence, then this sequence will follow:

Evidence-claim + explanation → inference

Where we have more than one explanation for evidence, then more than one inference could be drawn, depending on which explanation is used.

Evidence-claim + explanation 1 → inference 1

Evidence-claim + explanation 2 → inference 2

(and so on)

Where we have (and use) more than one explanation for evidence, then the inference will be drawn accordingly.

	+ explanation 1	↘	
Evidence-claim	+ explanation 2	→	inference
	+ explanation 3	↗	

In an important sense, inference must wait its turn until explanation allows it in. Explaining evidence-claims is necessary to give them a significance, which is then made concrete by inference.

We've now restored explanations to their rightful place at the heart of Critical Thinking. What we've seen is that, until we've looked at explanations, we very often can't do much with a claim.

What follows is an opportunity for you to do some explanation work with another evidence-claim.

Here's the evidence for you to consider.

35 per cent of US and 20 per cent of UK entrepreneurs are dyslexic.

What else do you need to know to see if this evidence is, in any way, significant?

If it is significant, what might be an explanation for it?

Given an explanation, is there any inference that could be drawn from it? (Therefore what?) (You can find some analysis to help you on p.112.)

3

INFERENCES

In the previous chapter we saw that, by looking at evidence-claims and their significance, we highlighted the importance of explanations. And, by highlighting explanations, we found that we opened the door to inference. Indeed, for inference to force its way in before explanations have opened the door risks inferences that have considerable problems.

This point is particularly well illustrated with predictions, where we find explanations have an especially important role. Indeed, with prediction-claims, explanations move forwards as the starting point, such that the prediction itself is the inference.

You will remember the example we gave in Chapter 1.

> There is a baby already born today that will live until it's 250.

You can see that this prediction can be viewed as an inference from claims that make up an explanation. This explanation is concerned with (presumably) changes in medical knowledge. These changes could be detailed to include greater understanding of genetic diseases and how to slow down the ageing process.

> There will be big changes in medical knowledge over the coming years which will enable us to cure far more diseases than we can at the moment, and which will mean that ageing can be very much slowed down. So, there is a baby already born today that will live until it's 250..

Here's another prediction.

> In 500 million years' time, there will be no plant life on Earth.

The prediction is again based on an explanation, this time that the Sun has been getting progressively hotter for millions of years and will continue to do so, such that its heat will eventually make plant life (and thus all life) on Earth impossible.

The prediction could then be used to support an inference.

> In 500 million years' time, there will be no plant life on Earth. So, at some point in the distant future, we have will have to abandon Earth and move to live on a different planet.

> Explanation → Prediction → Inference

We'll keep returning to this link between claims, explanations, and inferences. But, for the rest of this chapter, we're going to focus on the process of inference itself.

You'll remember that we represented the process of inference as claim → claim. The arrow sign shows that the second claim is being *drawn from* the first. Take out the arrow sign and we have just two separate claims. This shows the importance of the relationship between the two. It also shows that there is an important thing going on. Whoever draws the inference is saying that the first claim is enough for the second one to be drawn. We'll be coming back to this point time and time again throughout the book.

We'll now look at some examples of inference.

> The need for people to hug each other in today's world is understandable. So it is good that so many young people, both boys and girls, hug each other.

This is based on a letter to *The New York Times* in May 2009. Because we have the second claim drawn from the first, we have inference. In other words, we have an argument. The author is arguing that it's good that young people hug each other *because* there is an understandable need for people to hug each other. This shows that we can turn round the argument, without the direction of inference being changed.

> It is good that so many young people, both boys and girls, hug each other, because the need for people to hug each other in today's world is understandable.

In this way, we can see that, however the direction of the inference is presented, the argument as such remains the same.

Interestingly, we have here another example where the argument flows out of an explanation.

> Following 9/11, school shootings, and other tragedies that we see time and time again in the media, young people are increasingly aware of the fragility of life, of their own mortality. As a result, the need for people to hug each other in today's world is understandable. So it is good that so many young people, both boys and girls, hug each other.

The first sentence is an explanation (as used in the letter), and it's used here as support for the second sentence. In other words, we have here an example of

Claim (explanation) → claim (inference from explanation) → claim (inference from inference).

You can see how arguments can be built up, step by step.

Here's another argument on the same subject (based on another letter):

> Physical touch is an important human need. So it is good that so many young people, both boys and girls, hug each other.

In this argument, the same inference is drawn from a different claim.

By the way, you will have noticed that we've used the word 'argument' time and time again. At no point did we fret about what it isn't, so long as we understood what it is. An 'argument' might well be a disagreement, a quarrel, a debate. It might sometimes involve shouting or insults. We don't really care, as long as we remember that, for us, in this subject, an argument has to have the process of claim → claim going on. There has to be at least one claim being drawn from at least one other.

We've been using the word 'so' to indicate that an inference is going on (except when we reversed the sentences and connected them with a 'because'). You'll find lots of other words that can be used: *therefore, thus, in consequence, as a result, it follows that*. You might find that no words are used at all.

> Physical touch is an important human need. Therefore it is good that so many young people, both boys and girls, hug each other.

> Physical touch is an important human need. It is good that so many young people, both boys and girls, hug each other.

In the second version above, the inference can still be seen as the second claim being drawn from the first. Even though it's not actually there, a word like 'so' or 'therefore' sort of shouts at us to say 'I'm here' when we read the two sentences together.

Look at the next example.

> The use of sunbeds to get a tan should be banned. More than 10,000 people a year in the UK are developing malignant melanoma, the deadliest form of skin cancer, with sunbeds being one of the main causes.

What's going on here?

You will probably have spotted that the inference was given first. The claim that the use of sunbeds should be banned is drawn (inferred) from evidence on skin cancer and its link with sunbeds. An interesting thing is that no words such as 'so' (or 'because') were used, but there was a different word which gave us a big hint that an inference was being drawn. This was the word 'should'. Words like this – ought to, must, and their negatives shouldn't, ought not to, must not – often indicate that an inference has been drawn. Note the word 'often': these words don't *always* indicate an inference.

> We should not allow young people to use sunbeds. Therefore salons that allow them to do so need to be prosecuted.

In this example, though the first sentence contains the word 'should', it is the claim that's used to support the inference.

There was something else to note in the first version of the sunbed argument. Look at the second sentence again.

> The use of sunbeds to get a tan should be banned. More than 10,000 people a year in the UK are developing malignant melanoma, the deadliest form of skin cancer, with sunbeds being one of its main causes.

What we have in the second sentence are really two claims.

> More than 10,000 people a year in the UK are developing malignant melanoma, the deadliest form of skin cancer.

> Sunbeds are one of the main causes of malignant melanoma.

So what we have are two claims from which the inference is drawn:

> claim + claim → claim

If you look at this sentence, the inference certainly needs the second claim, although the first gives some extra significance to the second.

REASONS AND CONCLUSIONS

We're beginning to see how arguments are built up, piece by piece, claim by claim. It is probably a good time to introduce a refinement to the terms used in describing what's going on in arguments.

We have seen that the basic feature of an argument is that of a line of inference. A claim is inferred from another one. To distinguish which claims are doing what, we refer to them as either 'reasons' or 'conclusions'. The idea of a 'reason' should fit with how we've been looking at inference. You'll remember this example that we looked at a little earlier:

> It is good that so many young people, both boys and girls, hug each other, because the need for people to hug each other in today's world is understandable.

The word 'because' tells us that the second half of the sentence is the reason used to draw the inference in the first half. So we can see that is what's going on in the most basic type of argument:

> Claim (= reason) → claim

There's also a term that's used for the claim that's an inference. This is 'conclusion'. This term is appropriate because it's where the argument has ended up. It's the final destination. It's where the author of the argument wants to go.

The use of sunbeds to get a tan should be banned. More than 10,000 people a year in the UK are developing malignant melanoma, the deadliest form of skin cancer, with sunbeds being one of the main causes.

If we look again at this argument, though we saw that the inference was the first sentence, it was where the author wanted to go. It was the point that they wanted to make. In this way, then, the first sentence was what would be called the 'conclusion' of the argument. You might come across all sorts of ways of seeing this explained, but the simplest (and thus most effective) way of seeing what a conclusion is is to see it as the main point that the author wants to make. In the above example, you can see that the author's main point is to say that sunbeds should be banned. The evidence on skin cancer and the link between it and sunbeds are claims which help the author on their way.

Look at the next example. It should be pretty clear what's going on:

Parents need to control how their children use their mobile phones. Evidence has shown a recent doubling in the texts received and sent by teenagers, with an average of about 80 messages a day.

All we have is two claims, with the second one providing a reason for the first one. As you can see, the main point the author wants to make is the first sentence: this is the conclusion drawn from the evidence.

Before we move on, you will see that we're still very much looking at the significance of claims. The evidence-claim (second sentence) is given a significance by the author when the inference is drawn. Without this inference, the claim simply sits there with no necessary significance. When we come to look at assumptions in arguments, we'll be very much into this again.

Anyway, back to the short argument. We can show what's going on by labelling the passage.

(C) Parents need to control how their children use their mobile phones. (R) Evidence has shown a recent doubling in the texts received and sent by teenagers, with an average of about 80 messages a day.

Though the sequence in the argument is $C \leftarrow R$, we'd normally show the process of inference as $R \rightarrow C$.

We'll now add to this argument.

> Parents need to control how their children use their mobile phones. Evidence has shown a recent doubling in the texts received and sent by teenagers, with an average of about 80 messages a day. In many cases, teenagers are sending and receiving messages through the night, causing them to lose sleep.

We now have another evidence-claim. What is this doing? It's providing, in the third sentence, another reason for the conclusion. The author is arguing that the big increase in numbers of texts sent and received is the first reason for parents to control their children's use of phones. The effect on their children's sleep is the second. So we now have R + R → C. This is often shown as a vertical sequence.

$$R + R$$
$$\downarrow$$
$$C$$

There is a technical point that we can deal with here. We have given the structure of the argument as R + R → C (or in its other vertical form). But there is another way of showing this, which says something about the reasons themselves.

In this example, the reasons are what are called 'independent'. This means that they work separately, each one supporting the conclusion from a particular direction. A simple test to see how this works is to look at what would happen if a reason was removed. If it is an independent reason, the conclusion could still be drawn. We know that, in our example, the second reason could be taken out because we've already seen the conclusion drawn with just the first one. So what happens if we take out the first one?

> Parents need to control how their children use their mobile phones. In many cases, teenagers are sending and receiving messages through the night, causing them to lose sleep.

As you can see, it still works. So the reasons operate independently. We can show this independent reasoning in a particular way.

In this version, the lack of the + sign indicates that the conclusion doesn't need the two reasons added together. In addition, the way that the reasons do their work is shown by each reason having its own arrow, rather than one for both of them.

In the next example, we again have a conclusion drawn from two reasons.

(R) Teenagers have a great interest in knowing what's going on in the lives of their peers. (R) They will be very anxious if they're left out of the loop. (C) So the big increase in texting can be seen as both positive and negative.

You will be able to see that, in this argument, the conclusion needs both reasons. Just try it with only any one of them. You'll see that the first reason needs the second to arrive at an inference which sees texting as both negative and positive. The second reason highlights only a potentially negative aspect.

So here we don't have independent reasons. We have what are called 'joint' reasons. They work together. We show this working together by using the + sign.

$$R + R$$
$$\downarrow$$
$$C$$

It can also be shown with the reasons connected in the following way.

$$\underline{R + R}$$
$$\downarrow$$
$$C$$

Can we have arguments with a mixture of joint and independent reasons? Yes, we can.

Teenagers are supposed to increasingly break free from their parents during adolescence. Texting enables the teenager to keep in touch with their parents, about the smallest detail of their lives. Teenagers need peace and quiet in their lives to develop into the person they want to be. So the big increase in texting can be seen as restricting the psychological development of teenagers.

What's going on in this argument? We've got two lines of reasoning. The first two sentences work together to show one negative aspect of texting for the psychological development of teenagers. The third sentence comes in with a separate line of reasoning to show another negative aspect. The argument therefore combines both joint and independent reasons. We can show it in the following way.

$$\frac{R + R}{\searrow \swarrow} \quad R$$

$$C$$

Just to make sure that we've got this right, just try the argument by removing reasons. If we remove the third reason, what do we have?

> Teenagers are supposed to increasingly break free from their parents during adolescence. Texting enables the teenager to keep in touch with their parents, about the smallest detail of their lives. So the big increase in texting can be seen as restricting the psychological development of teenagers.

As you can see, the argument still works: the conclusion can still be drawn.

But what happens if we remove the first sentence?

> Texting enables the teenager to keep in touch with their parents, about the smallest detail of their lives. Teenagers need peace and quiet in their lives to develop into the person they want to be. So the big increase in texting can be seen as restricting the psychological development of teenagers.

The argument no longer works. The first sentence was needed for the second sentence to work as a reason (and vice versa).

There is another feature of showing the structure of an argument that we can introduce here. This is numbering the reasons. This time, whether or not the reasons are joint or independent isn't the point: all we do is to give each reason a number to show their position in the sequence of the argument.

(R1) Teenagers are supposed to increasingly break free from their parents during adolescence. (R2) Texting enables the teenager to keep in touch with their parents, about the smallest detail of their lives. (R3) Teenagers need peace and quiet in their lives to develop into the person they want to be. (C) So the big increase in texting can be seen as restricting the psychological development of teenagers.

$$R1 + R2 \qquad R3$$
$$\searrow \qquad \swarrow$$
$$C$$

We've just had an argument with three reasons. There is no limit to the number that you can have in an argument.

> A big problem with teenagers using text messaging so much is that studying is frequently being interrupted by receiving or sending texts. A related problem is the way that studying can be affected by the teenager simply *expecting* a text, so being unable to concentrate on their work. Another problem is that of thinking itself being interrupted by yet another text. Furthermore, the huge amount of texting can also cause physical damage to young people's thumbs, as a result of repetitive strain injury. There is also the issue of perceived popularity, in that children who are seen as not getting many texts are seen as less popular. For all these reasons, it would be good if texting became much less common with teenagers.

In this argument, we have five reasons supporting the conclusion. You will perhaps have noticed that they are five independent reasons.

It might be helpful to have a brief recap at this stage.

- When at least one claim is used to draw another one, we have what is called an 'argument'.

- In the process of inference, the claim from which another claim is drawn is the reason.

- In the process of inference, the claim which is drawn from another one is the conclusion.

- Any number of claims can be used as reasons to support a conclusion.

- Independent reasons provide separate support for a conclusion.

- Joint reasons provide support for a conclusion, acting together.

INTERMEDIATE CONCLUSIONS

There is one more feature of this process of inference which needs to be noted at this stage. We've seen that the process of inference can involve any number of reasons (so long as there's at least one). But, perhaps oddly, the process of inference can involve any number of conclusions too. The oddness of this comes from how we described a conclusion. We said 'it's where the argument has ended up. It's the final destination. It's where the author of the argument wants to go'. This does seem to directly contradict the idea that there can be more than one conclusion.

To resolve this apparent contradiction, we need to see arguments as a bit like a journey. If you're setting off to travel somewhere, you know where you want to end up, what should be your final destination. But you also know that you will pass through various places on the way. They are places you reach in order to get to where you want to go.

In this way, we can see that arguments might have inferences that are drawn on the way to drawing the final inference. Let's look again at an example we used earlier.

> Teenagers are supposed to increasingly break free from their parents during adolescence. Texting enables the teenager to keep in touch with their parents, about the smallest detail of their lives. Teenagers need peace and quiet in their lives to develop into the person they want to be. So the big increase in texting can be seen as restricting the psychological development of teenagers.

The conclusion of this argument could be used to draw a further inference.

> The big increase in texting can be seen as restricting the psychological development of teenagers. Therefore we should discourage teenagers from texting so much.

As you can see, what had been the conclusion of an argument has now become a reason for a conclusion in another. This is straightforward. After all, a conclusion is a claim that just happens to be used as an inference. But, because it's a claim, it can be used to draw an inference. And so it can go on, with claims leading to inference-claims, which lead to further inference-claims, with no necessary end to the sequence.

If we put the last argument back on to the previous one, we can see what's happening.

Teenagers are supposed to increasingly break free from their parents during adolescence. Texting enables the teenager to keep in touch with their parents, about the smallest detail of their lives. Teenagers need peace and quiet in their lives to develop into the person they want to be. So the big increase in texting can be seen as restricting the psychological development of teenagers. Therefore we should discourage teenagers from texting so much.

As we have seen, what was the conclusion of the argument has now become a reason for the new conclusion. But it's important to note that, though it's used as a reason to support the conclusion, it's still a conclusion drawn from the three reasons. Because it's now become a conclusion drawn on the way to another conclusion, it's called an *intermediate conclusion*. An intermediate conclusion is one that is drawn on the way to the final or main conclusion. (Or, because there might be more than one, we can say that intermediate conclusions are drawn on the way to the final or main conclusion.)

So what does the structure of this argument now look like?

$$\underline{R1 + R2} \qquad R3$$
$$\searrow \qquad \swarrow$$
$$IC$$
$$\downarrow$$
$$C$$

We discussed just above that there are no limits to the number of reasons in an argument. In that intermediate conclusions act as reasons, there must therefore be no limit to the number of intermediate conclusions in an argument. Of course there can be only one final or main conclusion. (You'll see that this is given in the structure by 'C' to distinguish it from the intermediate conclusions.)

There's another point that we need to consider here. Read the next version of this argument.

Teenagers are supposed to increasingly break free from their parents during adolescence. Texting enables the teenager to keep in touch with their parents, about the smallest detail of their lives. Teenagers need peace and quiet in their lives to develop into the person they want to be. So the big increase in texting can be seen as restricting the psychological development of teenagers. It is very important for teenagers to have the opportunity for proper psychological development. Therefore we should discourage teenagers from texting so much.

You will see that another claim has been put in between the intermediate conclusion and the main conclusion: *It is very important for teenagers to have the opportunity for proper psychological development.* What function does this claim perform? It can't be drawn as an inference from the intermediate conclusion. It does, however, act as a further reason from which the main conclusion is drawn. It was, as you might have spotted, sort of hanging in the air before we put it in. (This general point about reasons 'hanging in the air' will be looked at in detail in the next chapter.)

So, given that the new claim is a reason for the main conclusion, the structure of the argument will now look like this.

$$R1 + R2 \qquad R3$$
$$\searrow \qquad \swarrow$$
$$IC + R4$$
$$\downarrow$$
$$C$$

(You will see that IC and R4 operate as joint reasons.)

At this point, we now know how to unravel what's going on in argument. We can reveal the structure and thus make sense of the lines of inference. That's good, but we're now going to meet something that's part of the structure, but we have yet to see it. Weird? Read on.

4

ASSUMPTIONS

We have so far concentrated on looking at the process of inference in two ways. We've looked at what's involved in drawing an inference from a claim to create arguments. We've also looked at how arguments are put together, focusing on reasons and conclusions. In this way, we've got some understanding of how arguments work. Towards the end of the last chapter, however, we hinted that there might be something else going on. This was when we talked of a reason 'hanging in the air'. We're now going to look at such reasons in detail.

In looking at the process of inference, we see that someone judges that a claim is sufficient for an inference to be drawn. They have judged that the claim that supplies the reason (or claims that supply the reasons) justifies the conclusion being drawn. But it's very likely that they're relying on other reasons too, reasons that, as we have seen, are hanging in the air. Let's look at an example:

> The peak age for committing crime both in the UK and the US is 14–15 for girls and 17–18 for boys. We therefore need to put in place strong deterrents against committing crime for both of these groups.

This is a nicely simple argument. We have one reason (an evidence-claim) being used to draw one conclusion. The thrust of the argument is straightforward enough. Here are the age-groups that are a particular problem for crime, so we should target them with 'strong deterrents'. Simple yes, but you might have thought that there's quite a lot hanging in the air between the evidence-claim and the inference from it.

To uncover what's hanging there, go back to the point we made in the first chapter. An evidence-claim just sits there as a neutral claim unless and until someone comes along and says 'this evidence-claim has this significance'. This is no exception. And it's when the inference is added, as you know, that the significance is given.

So what significance has the author of this argument given the evidence-claim? The evidence, they think, shows that we can do something about the problem of crime, that it shows us a way forward: strong deterrents are the way forward.

But, when we look at the evidence, it didn't in itself show us that. So how has the author moved from an evidence-claim to a recommendation? By adding in all sorts of other claims, claims that are necessary to bridge the gap between 'here's the evidence' and 'here's what we should do about it'.

Let's look at one of these:

There are not already strong deterrents in place targeted at this age group.

You can see that, for the author to recommend that something should be done, they have to believe that this something hasn't already been done. In this example, though the author of the argument hasn't claimed that there aren't already deterrents in place, they must accept or believe that they're not.

So we've actually found another claim in the argument. Technically, it's another reason, because that's how it's doing its job. Put it into the argument to see why it *must* be there.

The peak age for committing crime both in the UK and the US is 14–15 for girls and 17–18 for boys. There are not already strong deterrents in place targeted at this age-group. We therefore need to put in place strong deterrents against committing crime for both of these groups.

What we have found is a missing reason, a reason that forms part of the argument, indeed a necessary part of the argument. But it's not stated. We have found what is called an *assumption*. The author has assumed this reason rather than stated it.

Let's see if there are any more of these assumed (unstated) reasons.

14–15-year-old girls and 17–18-year-old boys would be influenced by strong deterrents.

This has to be accepted by the author. As with the claim that there weren't already deterrents in place, it's a necessary part of the move from the evidence to the inference. If the author didn't believe this to be the case, then their inference doesn't follow. Let's put it into the argument and see how it fits well.

> The peak age for committing crime both in the UK and the US is 14–15 for girls and 17–18 for boys. There are not already strong deterrents in place targeted at this age group. 14–15-year-old girls and 17–18-year-old boys would be influenced by strong deterrents. We therefore need to put in place strong deterrents against committing crime for both of these groups.

Again, we can see that it is an essential part of the argument, essential in that it's a necessary reason for the conclusion that's been drawn.

Here's one more:

> There aren't better ways of reducing crime with these age groups than by using strong deterrents.

If the author thought there were better ways, then their conclusion is an odd one. Why recommend strong deterrents, when other methods would work better? So here's yet another additional, necessary reason.

> The peak age for committing crime both in the UK and the US is 14–15 for girls and 17–18 for boys. There are not already strong deterrents in place targeted at this age group. 14–15-year-old girls and 17–18-year-old boys would be influenced by strong deterrents. There aren't better ways of reducing crime with these age groups than by using strong deterrents. We therefore need to put in place strong deterrents against committing crime for both of these groups.

We've so far found three claims that the author of this argument had to accept as an essential part of their argument. A useful way of thinking about assumptions is to picture an X-ray machine at work. When we see a person (or animal), we see only so much, only what's presented to us. But when this person (or animal) stands in an X-ray machine, then we see much more. We see, in particular, their bones. When we see the skeleton, we realise that what we see on the outside is only part of the full picture. In fact, in all sorts of ways, what we see on the outside is only a small part. Without the skeleton, the body collapses.

This is what is going on when we look at an argument. We normally see only a small part of it. (This gives us another way of looking at what's going on with assumptions – think of them like the biggest part of the iceberg, the part that's hidden under the water.) When we look for assumptions, we're seeing so much more. We're seeing much more of the full content of the argument.

Let's just be sure as to what assumptions are.

● Assumptions are *reasons* in an argument.

● Assumptions are *unstated reasons* in an argument.

● Assumptions are *unstated but necessary reasons* in an argument.

Because assumptions are necessary reasons, this means that they're not to be confused with possible additional reasons that might be relevant to an argument but which are not required by it.

Here's an example:

> Using strong deterrents is the cheapest method of reducing crime with these age-groups.

If we put this into the argument, it serves well as a reason for the conclusion.

> The peak age for committing crime both in the UK and the US is 14–15 for girls and 17–18 for boys. There are not already strong deterrents in place targeted at this age group. 14–15-year-old girls and 17–18-year-old boys would be influenced by strong deterrents. There aren't better ways of reducing crime with these age groups than by using strong deterrents. Using strong deterrents is the cheapest method of reducing crime with these age groups. We therefore need to put in place strong deterrents against committing crime for both of these groups.

However, it is not *essential* for the conclusion. We know this because the author could still argue the way they do by believing it not to be true. Let's see this.

> The peak age for committing crime both in the UK and the US is 14–15 for girls and 17–18 for boys. There are not already strong deterrents in place targeted at this age group. 14–15-year-old girls and 17–18-year-old boys would be influenced by strong deterrents. Though using strong deterrents is not the cheapest method of reducing crime with these age groups, there aren't better ways of reducing crime with them than by using strong deterrents. We therefore need to put in place strong deterrents against committing crime for both of these groups.

So here we have an important point. An assumption isn't just relevant to an argument; it's essential to it. This distinction between relevant and essential is crucial in looking for assumptions.

Let's just return to the point we've just looked at, when we made the distinction between an essential reason in an argument and a relevant reason. You'll remember that we tested for essential or relevant by putting the opposite version of a claim in the argument. We found that, if the author could still argue the way they did with the opposite position in their argument, then the reason was not essential, therefore was not assumed. However, if the opposite version made the conclusion an inference that simply couldn't be drawn, then we have found an assumption. This is what is called 'the negative test' (a term I introduced some years ago). Let's use it on the argument we've been considering.

We'll put in the opposite of one of the assumed reasons we used earlier (shown in italics).

> The peak age for committing crime both in the UK and the US is 14–15 for girls and 17–18 for boys. There are not already strong deterrents in place targeted at this age group. *14–15-year-old girls and 17–18-year-old boys would not be influenced by strong deterrents.* We therefore need to put in place strong deterrents against committing crime for both of these groups.

This negative version now makes nonsense of the conclusion: strong deterrents wouldn't work, so introduce strong deterrents. You can see how, using the negative test, we can easily check whether a claim is assumed or not.

You might be wondering why it works. The answer is simple. Conclusions that are drawn from reasons that go in the opposite direction are rightly seen as nonsense (or odd, at the very least). It's a straightforward point that arguments should not contain what amounts to a contradiction.

> Finland has a very low imprisonment rate for young people. The UK has a relatively high one (although not as high as that of the US). Therefore, if the UK wants to increase its imprisonment rate for young people, it should learn how to do this from the Finns.

This, of course, stops you in your tracks. The conclusion goes the wrong way: presumably the UK could learn nothing from the Finns about how to increase the imprisonment rate for young people. Instead, given the evidence in the argument, the UK could perhaps learn from the US.

Assumptions are found not only in arguments. They're also found in explanations.

Denise Turner-Stewart was horrified at the graffiti in her local park. She wanted to do something about it so joined the Conservative Party and got herself nominated as a council candidate for Spelthorne in 2002 and won her borough council seat in 2003. (Surrey County Council website April 2009)

Here we read of what Ms Turner-Stewart did in response to the problem of graffiti in her local park. It is an explanation of why she decided to be a councillor. There are, however, missing parts of the explanation which are needed to make sense of it.

Getting action to reduce graffiti in her local park required being elected a councillor.

Being elected a councillor required membership of the Conservative Party.

Ms Turner-Stewart obviously slotted the second of these assumptions into her plan based on her understanding of the political reality of Surrey. In the 2009 elections, of the 80 councillors, 56 were Conservative and only one was Labour (with the rest divided between two other parties). Unfortunately, we don't know if the graffiti in her local park was reduced as a result of Denise's personal plan (but let's hope so).

It's important to note, before we move on, that finding assumptions in an argument is not an exercise in working out whether an argument's good or bad. It's a neutral exercise of finding missing reasons in an argument. When supposed experts tell you otherwise, they're wrong, simply wrong. It might well be that we can look at what an author has assumed and go on to ask questions about this, but that's not the same as simply finding them.

Here's an exercise to practise the finding of assumptions:

Find as many assumptions as you can in this argument. Use the negative test to check each one. (You can find some analysis to help you on p.113.)

Doing gymnastics in schools results in thousands of injuries to students a year. PE teachers need to be trained better in order to reduce the risk of injury to students as a result of doing gymnastics.

5

MORE BUILDING UP OF ARGUMENTS

At the end of Chapter 3 we had looked at arguments with more than one reason and more than one conclusion. We had worked out how to show the structure of these arguments. We're now going to start adding in some more possible parts and features of argument.

COUNTER-CLAIMS

Look at the next example:

> We are increasingly being told that the use of suncreams will protect our skin from the sun. However, there is a lot of evidence that suncreams might not work as well as they are supposed to. So we should be even more careful to ensure that we don't expose our skin to the sun for very long.

The argument is a very simple one. The second sentence provides the reason for the conclusion in the third sentence. So what is the significance of the first sentence? As you can see, it's referring to a claim that goes against the direction of the argument itself. This gives us the clue as to the significance of this first sentence. Another word for 'against' is 'counter' as in 'counter-terrorism'.

This first sentence is an example of what is called a *counter-claim*: it is a claim that goes against the main direction of the argument. So why is it there? It's because on occasions someone might choose to give the direction of the other side of the argument in order to lead us into their own argument. It can provide a context. 'Some people say this, but...' It can even have the function of giving emphasis to an argument. 'Some people say this, but I'm going to show why they're wrong.' It's a familiar method of arguing.

Sometimes the counter-claim is more developed.

> Suncreams with a high SPF (sun protection factor) such as 50+ are seen as providing very effective protection against being burned by the sun. Thus it is recommended that people should make sure that they use suncreams with an SPF of at least 50 (and preferably 70+) if they (and especially their young children) are out in the sun. However, this recommendation is a problem. Many suncreams have SPFs which are not accurate. In addition, people tend to put too little suncream on anyway, seriously reducing its effect.

What we now have is much more than a counter-claim being given. If you look at the first two sentences, they form an argument. The first sentence is the reason for the conclusion in the second. So instead of a counter-claim, we have a developed counter-argument. The author's actual argument comes after this. The conclusion is the third sentence supported by the two reasons that follow.

It's worth noting the use of the word 'however'. This often marks where an author is about to start their own argument having given a counter-position (claim or argument). This might also be marked by 'but' or 'on the other hand' or 'alternatively'.

In both examples, the author sets up the counter-position in order to knock it down. In many ways the counter-position is given to provide emphasis on its weakness. 'Here is a position; here are very good reasons why it should not be accepted.' Because of this, if there is a counter-position given, it will normally appear at the start of a short argument. It works better that way, given the way in which an author seeks to knock it down. In a longer argument, it could appear later but even then it will appear only to be knocked down.

We'll return to counter-claims and counter-arguments later when we're looking at both evaluation and production of arguments.

EVIDENCE AND EXAMPLES

As we have seen, a very common feature of arguments is the use of evidence, which is used to support the conclusion(s). The way in which this is used, however, can vary. We've already seen examples of where evidence has been used as a reason. Here's one we looked at in Chapter 3.

The use of sunbeds to get a tan should be banned. More than 10,000 people a year in the UK are developing malignant melanoma, the deadliest form of skin cancer, with sunbeds being one of the main causes.

We saw this as a simple piece of argument in which the conclusion (first sentence) is drawn from one reason (second sentence). In this example, the reason was no more than a piece of evidence (or, as we discussed, two pieces of evidence).

But what's happening in this next example?

Suncreams are often given inaccurate SPFs (four popular suncreams labelled as SPF15 were actually shown to provide an SPF of only 9 to 12), so people shouldn't think that they are necessarily protected from sunburn when they use them.

In this argument, the author is arguing that, since suncreams are often given inaccurate SPFs, people shouldn't think that using them will necessarily protect them. So what's the function of the specific evidence/examples given in the brackets?

It obviously provides some support for the claim that suncreams are often given inaccurate SPFs. It isn't a separate reason but is it a necessary part of the reasoning? The answer is clearly no: it strengthens the force of the reason but is not necessary for the reasoning. So here we have an example where an evidence-claim is not being used as a reason but acts merely to support a wider evidence-claim.

You will have seen that we've used both 'evidence' and 'example' in looking at the content of arguments. Is there a difference between the two? The answer is both yes and no. Let's see how.

Examples are straightforwardly a type of evidence. To try to hold the line between them, as if examples are not evidence, is a fool's errand. Now you'll find some fools in the world of Critical Thinking (as in other worlds), but we don't want to run their errands for them.

Let's say that we wanted to use evidence on health care in southern African nations to argue about the way in which what's spent on health care is a crucial aspect of people's health. Let's say that, in this argument, you gave evidence on Swaziland as a country with a poor health record and poor levels of spending. What's the difference between the evidence on southern African nations and that on Swaziland? Only that of the scope of the two. Evidence on Swaziland is, if you like, an example of the wider evidence. But then so too is the example of southern African states an example of evidence on all of Africa. And, of course, evidence on Africa is an example of evidence on all countries. So, as you can see, the distinction between the two keeps slipping through our fingers.

Sometimes examples can be used as reasons; sometimes evidence can be used as reasons; sometimes they can both support reasons. It all depends on how they're being used.

> The destruction of much of the European Jewish populations in the Holocaust demonstrates how easy it can be for ordinary people (shopworkers, teachers, clerks, postal workers, and so on) to carry out unbelievable cruelties against others. We must seek to educate people about the Holocaust so that nothing like it can ever happen again.

In this argument, we have evidence on the Holocaust used to draw a conclusion about 'nothing like it'. Within the evidence there are examples given. At two levels, then, we have examples. The second is pretty obvious – examples of 'ordinary people' are given. The first is the use of the evidence of the Holocaust itself. It could be seen as an example of 'unbelievable cruelties'. In this argument the evidence of the Holocaust is used as the reason for the conclusion. The examples of ordinary people are not used as a reason, but to give emphasis. (How can a postal worker shoot pregnant women, smash a child's head against a wall, kick an old person to death?)

You can see how this same argument could go through a number of layers and yet still be arguing for the same thing.

> The destruction of much of the Polish Jewish people (including those in Warsaw, Krakow, and Lodz) in the Holocaust demonstrates how easy it can be for ordinary people (shopworkers, teachers, clerks, postal workers, and so on) to carry out unbelievable cruelties against others. We must seek to educate people about the Holocaust so that nothing like it can ever happen again.

> The destruction of so many Jewish families in the Holocaust demonstrates how easy it can be for ordinary people (shopworkers, teachers, clerks, postal workers, and so on) to carry out unbelievable cruelties against others. We must seek to educate people about the Holocaust so that nothing like it can ever happen again.

The death of Anne Frank in the Holocaust is of course a well-known example of the tragedy of this event. Though she is only one example amongst millions of others, we could write this argument using her story as a reason.

> The death of Anne Frank shows how ordinary people can carry out unbelievable cruelties against others. Though she was only a defenceless girl, she suffered hugely in the camps where she was taken. We must seek to educate people about the Holocaust so that nothing like it can ever happen again.

As we can see, arguments can use evidence (including examples) in all sorts of ways. In fact, a very high proportion of arguments have a combination of evidence (including examples) and inference.

Having spent a little time looking at the role of evidence in arguments, we're now going to look in some detail at how we might evaluate this evidence.

EVALUATION OF ARGUMENTS: LOOKING AT EVIDENCE

We have spent some time peering into arguments, asking questions like, 'What's going on here?' It's time now to move beyond these questions and to start to ask the question, '*Should* this be going on?'

We've looked at lots of examples where the author is saying here are my reasons for arguing this. These examples might look as if they're an equation in which R+R = C. But most examples you'll come across (and use) won't be like an equation.

> In a recent UK survey, 61 per cent of the people who took part in it said that they were not prepared to pay for the upkeep of the Royal Family. Therefore most people in the UK are not prepared to pay for the upkeep of the Royal Family.

In this example, the reason (the evidence-claim) is not equivalent to the inference drawn from it. You can see that the shift from 61 per cent of people who took part in the recent UK survey to 'most people in the UK' is quite a jump. It might well be that the survey was a very good indicator of the attitude of people on this subject. However, for various reasons, it might not. Perhaps the survey wasn't accurate. We'll return to this general point below.

VALID ARGUMENTS

The most we could have said about the inference in this argument was that it was *probably* true. This, as we'll see time and time again, is the most we can say about the sort of arguments you'll come across. If you want certainty rather than just probability, you'll have to find (or use) arguments with a particular structure.

No vegetarians eat meat.

Martha Phillips is a vegetarian.

So Martha Phillips doesn't eat meat.

The argument is set out like this to emphasise what's going on. You should be able to see that, if the first two claims are true, then the inference (the third sentence) must also be. It isn't that it probably follows: it *must* follow. It must follow for the same reason that the negative test worked in finding assumptions: arguments should not be self-contradictory. It would be nonsense to infer that Martha Phillips eats meat, given the first two claims.

We have here an example of what's called a *syllogism*. These forms of argument always have two reasons which together (so joint reasons) lead to the conclusion. Specifically, you'll note that each reason has a term (words) in common with the conclusion, and one term (words) in common with the other reason. Looking at our example, let's see how this has worked there.

No *vegetarians* eat **meat**.

Martha Phillips is a *vegetarian*.

So *Martha Phillips* doesn't eat **meat**.

This particular argument was very strong (in fact, watertight) because of the way in which it was presented. But it was strong only if the reasons are true. If Martha Phillips has abandoned her vegetarianism, then the second claim isn't true, meaning the inference collapses.

When the reasons are true in an argument like this, then we have what is called a *valid* argument. Some arguments might look as if they're valid but, if the reasons aren't true, then they won't be valid.

It's useful to see how, in the valid argument above, the conclusion was, so to speak, contained within the reasons. It didn't go any further than what was supplied by them. In this way, it can be seen as an equation R+R=C.

However, if we look again at our argument on the Royal Family, we can see that the conclusion isn't contained within the reason: it goes further. Part of what's going on, of course, is that it goes further because there are other reasons being assumed. Our Martha Phillips argument didn't contain assumptions; the reasons supplied everything that was needed.

As we have before, we're now going to concentrate on looking at lots of arguments in which the reasons don't supply everything, where the inference has moved to a greater or lesser extent beyond them. As we have seen above, you're not likely to have to deal with any other sort of argument. So remember, the most that we can expect from the arguments that we're likely to find is that the conclusion *probably* follows from the reason(s).

QUESTIONING THE SIGNIFICANCE OF CLAIMS

We have already met quite a few arguments where it is evidence-claims that supply the reasons. You will remember that, in the first chapter, we spent some time looking at such claims (including those of statistical evidence) and kept asking the question 'what is the significance of this claim?' We'll look now at lots more evidence and we'll keep asking that question.

Statistical evidence is very commonly used in arguments. It's often seen as a particularly powerful part of the reasoning, perhaps because numbers give a good impression of 'facts'.

When adverts for cosmetics are shown on TV, they often provide in a small font in the bottom left- or right-hand corner of the screen some statistical evidence.

Of 97 women, 72 agreed that wrinkles were less visible.

This sort of evidence is meant to support the other claims being made in the advert. These will be something like, 'Our age-rejection cream will make you look years younger.' Perhaps it will, but does the evidence support the claim? If so, to what extent?

You might want to discuss the significance of 'less visible'. This does not have to mean 'invisible'. It could mean no more than, at first glance, wrinkles are (a little) less noticeable than before. In addition, you might want to look at the numbers involved. Why 97? Who were they? How were they chosen? Over what time period did they use the cream? Did they use it, or did they merely observe its effect on others who did? Did they all use the term 'less visible' in the same way – that is, in the same situations (amount of light available, degree of wrinkled skin, and so on)? It could be, for example, that tiny wrinkles become less visible but deeper ones are not visibly affected. And what about the 25 who didn't notice the difference? Why didn't they?

The evidence is meant to operate as a reason for the inference given in the advert. Accordingly, you will probably have spotted an assumption here.

> Of 97 women, 72 agreed that wrinkles were less visible. (*Less visible wrinkles will make you look years younger.*) Our age-rejection cream will make you look years younger.

That's quite a big assumption and is itself open to questions of meaning. How much 'less visible'? (Can it be quantified into a percentage?) How many 'years younger'? (Two, three...?)

We've just looked at some very specific evidence ('of 97 women...'). But often evidence can be presented in a much more general way.

> The taller a man is, the higher his income is likely to be, and the better his promotion chances are.

This time there are no numbers, no percentages, nothing beyond the giving of a correlation between a man's height and his income and promotion chances. So what sort of inference could be drawn from this sort of evidence?

> The taller a man is, the higher his income is likely to be, and the better his promotion chances are. So employers discriminate against short men when it comes to pay and promotion/short men lack the confidence to further their careers/there needs to be a policy making heightism illegal.

We have reached an important point. Which of these inferences does the evidence-claim best support (if any)? We'll introduce here a way of looking at this problem. This is to look at the process of inference in terms of a bank account.

We know that we can spend only what is in our bank account (ignoring loans, credit cards, gifts, and so on). If we spend more, then we are overdrawn. We have literally taken out of the account more than was in there. The link with inference is a simple one. The claim(s) from which an inference is drawn represent(s) what is in the account. You can therefore infer (spend) no more than what the claim(s) permit(s).

Let's return to the evidence on men's height. We gave three possible inferences. Can we afford any of these? Interestingly, if this evidence is a general trend (which it seems to be), then something appears to be going on which needs explaining. You will again see, by the way, that explanations are never far away in Critical Thinking (whatever some might say or write). Without an explanation, we don't really know what's going on here. So what inference we can afford depends on what explanation we put into the account. Without it, there's not enough in there to go straight from the evidence to an inference. Let's see why.

> The taller a man is, the higher his income is likely to be, and the better his promotion chances are. So employers discriminate against short men when it comes to pay and promotion.

The inference has taken too much out of the account: transaction declined. Quite simply, we don't know from just the evidence why taller men do better. To make this inference, we need to add something into the account.

> The taller a man is, the higher his income is likely to be, and the better his promotion chances are. Employers see shorter men as being less competent at their job. So employers discriminate against short men when it comes to pay and promotion.

Has this addition to the account given us enough to spend on the inference? It's certainly taken us away from being as overdrawn as we before. But there's still a worry that the case hasn't been fully established. We know that taller men earn and get promoted more, and that the author claims that employers see shorter men as being less competent *but* (yes, there's a pronounced but) we don't know if these two claims together show/demonstrate (prove, if you like) that the better pay and promotion chances of taller men are *as a result of* how employers see shorter men. So there's still a big hint of overdrawn here.

Perhaps taller men (for whatever reason) are better qualified, healthier (so take less time off sick), have happier home lives (so work more contentedly and consistently), or whatever. To show how the picture can indeed be muddied by such possibilities, there is evidence (by Danish researchers on shorter British men) that such short men reported worse physical and mental health than those of 'normal' height. In addition, a French study has found that men who are 6ft or more tall are 50 per cent more likely to be married or in a long-term relationship than men who are 5ft 5in or below.

We can see then that drawing any inference from our first claim starts to look very difficult. Let's just have a look at the third inference.

> The taller a man is, the higher his income is likely to be, and the better his promotion chances are. So there needs to be a policy making heightism illegal.

There is an organisation called the National Organisation of Short Statured Adults (NOSSA) which argues that what it calls 'heightism' should indeed be made illegal. The famous and brilliant economist J K Galbraith (6ft 8in) referred to it as 'one of the most blatant and forgiven prejudices in our society.' But does the evidence enable us to make the inference above?

Of course, assumptions are never far away, and there's at least one assumption needed to connect the evidence with the inference.

> The explanation for taller men tending to have higher pay and better promotion chances is that there is prejudice by employers against short men.

> The effects of the prejudice against short men by employers over pay and promotion could be at least lessened by making heightism illegal.

So, it's the same story. The original claim and inference didn't work without the inference being overdrawn. But would the two assumptions we've just identified stop the inference being overdrawn, if they were turned into stated reasons?

They're certainly effective in dealing with the issue of what causes taller men to do better in pay and promotion (so they close off concerns about why shorter men do less well). But the inference is still overdrawn. We would also need the claim that having a prejudice against short men is not a good thing. Going back to our earlier point about whether there are health-related causes of heightism, we would need the claim that the explanation for heightism is not to do with factors that would stop short people from getting on well at work.

You might be thinking by now that we can't ever infer anything safely once we stray out of the enclosed world of the valid syllogism. But this would be to cut us off from the normal way in which we argue. What we've seen is that inferences are normally, at best, only probably true. The claims that are used to support inferences might take us a long way towards certainty, but will never quite get there. But in Critical Thinking we are not normally after certainty: an inference with a high probability of being true would sit nicely at our table.

IMPLICATIONS

Having talked a lot about strong claims and inferences, it's interesting to note that sometimes claims are left deliberately weak, although the intended message of the assumed inference is meant to be strong.

> You could save money with our price comparison website.

This claim is, of course, entirely compatible with another one.

> You might not save money with our price comparison website. (Or even 'you will not save money...')

But you're meant to draw the inference from the first one that 'it would be a good idea to use this price comparison website'. You're not meant to do anything with the other claim. It sits there uninvited. It was us that let it into the discussion.

Just a little diversion before we move on. When we referred to an 'assumed inference' above, we were in fact looking at what is technically called an *implication*. There was no inference drawn from the claim, but the given claim was designed such that you *would* draw a particular one. We could ask 'What was implied by the claim?' and the answer is, 'The implication is that you should use the website'. Though the implication that you wouldn't save money is also there, it's in a way being jostled out of the picture by the context in which the claim appears. The advert in which it appears is not a neutral context in which claims are being presented for neutral discussion. It's not as if Socrates is toying with the idea that he could save money on his insurance by using a price comparison website and responds with the counter-claim that he also could not.

Watch out for claims (especially evidence-claims) that just sit there with an intended implication sitting next to them. Here's a recent evidence-claim:

> TV reduces adult-child conversations.

This claim appeared in a June 2009 edition of *The New York Times*. The implication that is sitting next to it is not 'so parents should have the TV on more when they're with children'. It is, of course, the opposite. Once again, as we have seen, we're back to the point about the significance of claims. We've stressed time and time again that claims have a neutral significance unless and until someone comes along and gives them a particular significance. So, an alien from a planet which has been searching for ways of getting children to talk less to adults would be thrilled by the finding and report back from New York to alien HQ that every household on the planet must have the TV on much more. Implication becomes inference when someone draws the implication.

When looking at evidence-claims, are some types less problematic than others? Let's look at some of them.

PERCENTAGES

Percentages are often seen as particularly useful because they deal with the possible problem of the disputable significance of overall numbers. Thus, the information that, for every hour that the TV is on, there is a seven per cent decrease in the number of words that a child hears is probably more helpful than knowing that the child hears 770 fewer words. The overall number might seem more dramatically significant but the problem is knowing how significant it really is.

There can, however, be issues of significance with percentages. These are found especially when we are looking at percentages involving small numbers. Look at the next argument:

> At the fifth Teenage Cancer Trust conference held in June 2008, it was reported that between 1979 and 2003, the incidence of cervical cancer had increased by 1.6 per cent per year. But the figure for those aged 15–19 was 6.8 per cent per year. These figures show that it is the increase in teenagers with the disease that is causing the overall increase. Therefore we need to have a campaign to educate teenagers about the dangers of having lots of sexual partners.

You can see that the author gives us two different percentages. Both refer to percentage changes over the period 1979–2003. In this way, they might be seen as comparable. In one important way, they are. But might there be a problem in comparing the two? The first covers cases of cervical cancer in all age groups in the

UK over a 14-year period. The second covers only the 15–19 age group. This alerts us to why there might be a problem. Obviously the 15–19 age group is significantly smaller in number than that of all age groups (15 to 100+). In addition, we would expect very few 15–19 females to get cervical cancer (indeed, to get any form of cancer). And this turns out to be a devastatingly significant point. It has been calculated that a 6.8 per cent increase in cervical cancer per year for the 15–19 age group represents an actual number of 0.1 to 0.2 cases a year. This means that a 6.8 per cent increase is equivalent to one or two cases every ten years!

So when the CEO from the Teenage Cancer Trust said, 'It is worrying that cervical cancer . . . (is) increasing in teenagers faster than in other groups. More education is desperately needed so young people can change their behaviour before it's too late', we would say, beware of drawing the wrong inference from percentages. (He was also talking about melanoma, an issue we considered when we were looking at sunbeds and suncreams.)

There was a similar problem when Critical Thinking was described as the 'fastest-growing A-level in Britain' a few years ago. This was easily explained. Because it started off from such a low figure, it was easy to be the fastest-*growing* A-level!

So when we're given evidence-claims in the form of a percentage, working out their significance is a task where we need to tread with care.

- What is the number from which the percentage is calculated?

- When comparing percentages of different groups, are the numbers themselves sufficiently comparable?

In addition, when we're looking at percentage changes over a given timescale, we need to ask these questions:

- *Is the timescale itself problematic?* For example, a timescale could be selected because it fits with the author's position by emphasising a particular percentage increase or decrease.

- *What sort of percentage change would we expect, if there was no significant difference from one period to another?* We have to be careful here. It could well be that we would expect an increase or decrease anyway, for all sorts of reasons.

Overall truancy rates rose to 1.1 per cent in the Spring term of 2009 compared to 1 per cent for the same term of 2008.

Is this significant? The schools spokesman for the Liberal Democrat Party must have thought so, because he described the figures as 'a disgrace. The Government's truancy strategies are not working. Ministers have poured hundreds of millions of pounds into reducing truancy over recent years but this money seems to have been completely wasted.' (*The Times*, 27 August 2009)

Our response, as Critical Thinkers, would be to say, 'Now hold on, David Laws, we need to think more carefully about this. Is a 0.1 per cent increase significant? Does it tell us that the money spent on reducing truancy has been "completely wasted"? What sort of percentage figure are you looking for? Zero per cent? We don't know what the truancy percentage would have been without the truancy strategies, so perhaps a 0.1 per cent increase is pretty good. Do we need to know what the figure was for years earlier than 2008? Was 2008 an unusually low figure, so that a small increase in 2009 is actually pretty good?'

And so on. Quite simply, percentages can be very slippery customers, with their significance sliding through our fingers as we try to grab hold of it. We very often need to know much more before we can start drawing useful inferences.

REAL NUMBERS

So, what about real numbers? Instead of percentages, what about the numbers from which they're taken? Do they give us the opportunity to hold on to something much more significant?

Look at the next example:

Britain spends a higher amount on cosmetic surgery than any other country in Europe. In 2006 this was £497m. The second highest was Italy with £158m. In fact, if we add up the total amount spent by the countries that were second, third (France), fourth (Germany), and fifth (Spain) in the league table of spending, this total is still less than the amount spent in Britain. This shows that British people are the vainest in Europe.

There's a lot of possible evaluation we could do with this argument, especially in terms of alternative explanations giving us different significances for the evidence.

53

One of the evaluation questions we might want to ask is population size. Perhaps the UK population size is sufficiently large to (partly) explain the UK's position in the European league table. A quick look at the numbers suggests not.

The population of the UK is 59.8m; that of Italy is 58.1m; France is 60.7m; Germany is 82.7m; with the only one noticeably lower than the UK being Spain with 43.4m.

There would have been little point translating these numbers into percentages: the numbers give us the information we need to see that it is not population size that in itself explains what's going on. (You still, of course, need to consider alternative explanations in relation to the inference. There are quite a few.)

Another example in which numbers themselves give us lots of information is the amount of time spent watching TV. The US tops the international league table here with an average daily household viewing of a little over eight hours. (Second is Turkey with five hours, with the UK way down the table on only three.) There would be no point in translating hours per day into a different measure, given that the number of hours per day does not change.

However, sometimes numbers might express something, but we're not sure what. For example, we know that the number of aid workers killed in 2008 whilst on duty was 140. In 2007, it was 75; in 2006 it was 84. So there was a big increase in aid workers (especially locally-recruited ones) being killed whilst working in 2008. Is this significant? Here we would need to know whether the number of aid workers has increased overall before we could infer something like 'the risk of death for aid workers has increased'.

Sometimes there's a further way of expressing the possible significance of a numerical claim. This is in the form of a rate. A percentage is a type of rate, expressed as a proportion per hundred. But we can find rates expressed as proportions of larger (sometimes much larger) numbers. When we are dealing with very large numbers, a rate (say, per 10,000, 100,000, or more) makes the possible significance of the information more approachable.

For example, does it tell us very much to read that the US spent $607.3 billion on defence in 2008? It tells us something because, by any standards, that's a lot of money. Is this figure given greater significance when we see that this amount represented 41.5 per cent of the total spent on defence in the world? Probably yes, because we can see that, given this percentage, the US will realistically be the biggest spender on defence of any country in the world.

But there's another measure which gives us a different significance. This is the amount spent on defence in $000s per person in a country's population. Using that rate measure, the US is not top of the league table. This position is held by Israel. Though Israel spends (only) $16.2 billion on defence, this represents about $2,300 per person in the country. (The US spends almost $2000 per person.) This league table of spending per person creates a very different picture from the overall amount and the percentage figures. For example, China is second in the list of percentage of global defence spending (with 5.8 per cent of all spending) but features nowhere in the top 15 spenders by rate per head of population (because of its massive population). Using this rate measure, a country like Brunei appears in the premier league of defence spenders, though it spends only $0.3 billion on defence.

Another rate that can be used is that per person in a group or country. Using this measure shows us that Greece heads the international cigarette smoking league table, with a little over eight cigarettes a day being smoked per person. At one level, this tells us a lot, although using this particular measure doesn't tell us everything. For example, the French come out 62nd in the league table, with only a little over two cigarettes per person. However, the French figure doesn't include the 20 per cent of cigarettes sold illegally, so it looks lower than it really is. This last example shows that a per person rate can be distorted by inadequate information. A further illustration is that of India which barely registers on the per person cigarette smoking scale. It comes in as 119th out of 123 countries surveyed. However, tobacco consumption is much higher than this evidence suggests, in that people in India have a fondness for chewing tobacco rather than smoking it.

So we can see that the way in which statistical evidence is presented can affect its possible significance. It will not surprise us, then, to see that such evidence is often used to serve an author's interest. This can be done, for example, by picking a particular year as the starting point for a percentage change comparison in order to produce an artificially low or high change. It can be done by ignoring (or playing down the significance of) counter-evidence, a method called 'cherry-picking'. This could be going on with the climate change debate, with different pieces of statistical evidence being used on both sides, such that there is evidence to support the claim that climate change is happening, and that it isn't.

Sometimes numbers can have a manufactured significance. If we look at the numbers of deaths of troops in military campaigns, what significance do they have? At the Battle of the Somme in 1916, something like 432,000 British troops were killed. Something like 500,000 German troops were killed. Was this more than expected?

Was this an acceptable number? In recent military campaigns (such as in Afghanistan), a casualty rate of more than one a day is seen as significant (and even one a day is). In *The Times* of 29 September 2009, Martin Barrow refers to 'appalling casualties' in the war in Afghanistan. How would he then have described the casualty rate of the Somme or at the battle for Stalingrad? What casualty rate wouldn't then appal? No casualties at all? Just ten or twenty?

Beware of the manufactured significance of numbers. Much of what is reported in the news has this significance. Numerical claims, like other claims we've been looking at throughout the book, take on a significance only when something is done with them.

7

EVALUATION OF ARGUMENTS: WEAKNESSES IN REASONING

In the previous chapter, we focused on the limits (and possibilities) of numerical evidence for inference. We established the point that inferences are normally only probably rather than certainly true. In this chapter we're going to continue this theme of evaluating the relationship between claims and inferences from them.

CORRELATION AND CAUSATION

In their book *The Joy of Laziness* (2005) Peter and Michaela Axt consider the example of Jim Fixx who was the pioneer of jogging. Before Jim Fixx, people who you saw running in the street were normally late for something. The line in *Forrest Gump* when Forrest says, 'I just felt like running, so I ran', would have made little sense to the pre-Fixx era (which was, of course, the point). So why is Jim Fixx being discussed in a book entitled *The Joy of Laziness*? Because he died at the age of 52.

You can perhaps already see the connection. Jim Fixx does a lot of jogging, and drops dead at the relatively young age of 52, therefore jogging is bad for your health. It's an example of $R+R \rightarrow C$.

Straightforwardly, the Axts are seeing jogging as at least highly relevant to Jim Fixx's death. They make the point that this sort of exercise is supposed to give some protection against heart disease, but hadn't with Fixx. (He died of a heart attack just after a race.) In that we've already considered the issue of the alternative explanation, you will have seen that here we have a good example. The authors have assumed that there is no alternative explanation beyond jogging for Jim's death. But you could, no doubt, think of others. (There's also the point that jogging might have extended his life, if he had had a heart condition that was improved by running.)

We have an example here of the often disputed issue of whether, because things are correlated, one must have caused the other. As you might know, when two things are correlated, it means that as one of the things changes in a particular way (increases, for example), then the other changes in a similar or opposite direction. Changes in a similar direction will show a positive correlation; changes in the opposite direction will show a negative correlation.

All sorts of things might correlate. The success of a national football team and the birth rate is one example. (Try to think this one through.) But just because things might correlate doesn't mean that there is a necessary causal relationship between them. Here's an example of correlation.

> Sales of expensive cosmetic treatments such as those made by L'Oréal (Lancôme and Yves Saint Laurent) declined significantly in 2009. At the same time, there was a big increase in the number of people having Botox treatment. People were obviously switching from spending on expensive cosmetic treatments to having Botox instead.

In this example, the author takes two pieces of evidence that are (negatively) correlated. The decline in expensive cosmetic treatments took place during a time when there was an increase in Botox treatments. However, the author infers that there is not just a correlation here, but also a causal relationship: the decline in the use of expensive cosmetics led to an increase in the use of Botox (and/or vice versa). This, of course, might indeed be the case. But what the author hasn't considered (at least as they have presented the argument) is that there might be an alternative explanation for what happened. For example, perhaps the decline in the use of expensive cosmetic treatments was caused by consumers seeing cheaper products as being as effective as the more expensive ones. (Indeed there is evidence of women increasingly choosing cheap face creams.) In this case, the increase in the use of Botox could be explained in other ways. (Perhaps because it became so widely available now in a range of clinics, salons, and even some dental surgeries.)

In this argument the author took it that, since there was a correlation between the decline in the use of expensive cosmetics and the increase in Botox, there was a causal relationship going on. As we have seen, this might not be the case. In this example, the author has used the words 'at the same time' to show the relationship between the two. This way of arguing has a particular name. It's a Latin term: *cum hoc, ergo propter hoc*. This means 'with (at the same time as) this, therefore because of this'. It's normally abbreviated to simply *cum hoc* (with 'cum' pronounced as 'come' and 'hoc' pronounced to rhyme with 'sock').

It's important to point out that *cum hoc* arguments might be perfectly acceptable. When we take money out of a cash machine and our account then has less money in it, the bank can straightforwardly argue that the cash machine withdrawal caused our account to have less money in it. So, though *cum hoc* arguments can be a problem (given at least one alternative explanation), they are not always.

A more familiar variation of this possible problem of correlation but not necessarily causation is shown in the following example.

> In the UK there has been a big increase in interest in health, fitness, and fashion among many young males in their 20s. They want to find out how to get and then stay in shape. They also want information on style and careers. As a result of this increase in interest, there has been an increase in the readership of magazines such as *Men's Health*. There has also been a decline in the readership of various 'lad mag' titles such as *FHM*, *Zoo*, and *Nuts*. Therefore young men are far more interested in looking after their own bodies than looking at pictures of those of minor TV and film actresses.

You will see that, in this argument, there are two correlations presented, with two causal relationships given. The first is the positive correlation between an increase in young men's interest in health, fitness, style and careers, with an increase in the readership of health magazines. The second is the negative correlation between this interest and the decline of 'lad mags'. The first correlation is seen as showing a cause and effect relationship ('as a result'): the increase in interest in health, etc., has caused the increase in the readership. The second correlation is used to draw the conclusion. Because young men are interested in health, etc., they are less interested in looking at pictures of young women.

We have here two examples of a well-known relative of *cum hoc*. This has an almost identical Latin term: *post hoc, ergo propter hoc*. ('Post' pronounced as in letters.) This translates as 'after this, therefore because of this'. In other words, *y* followed/came after *x*, therefore *x* caused *y*. You can see how the previous argument is very much a *post hoc* argument. But is it a weak argument?

The first correlation might be OK, but it could have a problem. The author sees the causal relationship as working from interest in health to increase in readership. But it could be the other way round. Perhaps the increase in the readership caused (or at least contributed to) the increase in interest in health, etc. Perhaps it's a bit of both. So the relationship between the two things might not be as the author has presented it.

The second correlation is also possibly problematic. In part, it's problematic because of the problems with the first. The author argues that

increase in interest in health etc. → increase in health magazines → decrease in lad mags.

(Their argument could also be seen as

increase in health, etc.

↘   ↙

increase in health magazines   decrease in lad mags).

But, whichever way we present it, the possible problem remains. Perhaps the decrease in lad mags is as a result of something else. For example, perhaps the pictures of minor actresses are easily available on the internet, for free.

Here we come back to a familiar issue: the possibility of an alternative explanation. You can see that, in this argument, the author had to assume that there weren't alternative useful explanations.

Whenever we're looking at these correlation and causation situations, we're faced with at least six possibilities:

- x caused y

- y caused x

- a third factor (z) caused x or y (and correlates with the other)

- a number of 'third' factors ($z1$, $z2$...) caused x or y

- x and y are both causes of each other

- x and y are correlated coincidentally

Let's look at an example which brings in the first five possibilities.

Recent research has shown that children who spend a lot of time (1.5 to 5.5 hours a day) watching TV have higher blood pressure than those who don't.

This applies even if the children are thin and get plenty of exercise. So we should ensure that children don't watch TV for more than an hour a day.

You can see the causation issue here is the relationship between TV-watching and blood pressure. Applying this to our five possibilities, we have the following:

- TV-viewing caused high blood pressure.

- Children with high blood pressure watch more TV.

- Children watch TV eating snacks (such as those with a high salt content) which cause high blood pressure.

- Some TV programmes are distressing to children, causing them to have higher blood pressure (rather than watching TV as such being the cause); watching a lot of TV might reduce the amount of (or disrupt the) sleep children have, leading to higher blood pressure.

- Watching TV raises blood pressure; raised blood pressure causes children to be more sedentary, so increasing the amount of TV watched.

In the argument, the author concluded that we should ensure that children don't watch TV for more than an hour a day. This conclusion was drawn by assuming that the second of the above possibilities wasn't the explanation for the evidence. The author might assume the first, the third, and fourth. But the third seems unlikely because the conclusion would then be something like 'we must ensure that children don't eat snacks while watching TV'. Even the fourth one has potential problems. If the author believed this to be the case, then the conclusion would be something like 'we must ensure that children do not watch distressing TV programmes' or 'we must ensure that we don't allow TV-watching to affect children's sleep'. (Though, to be fair to the author, they might have meant this when they gave their rather more general conclusion.)

As you can see, if the author leaves the explanation for the correlation assumed rather than stated, then we need to look carefully at the wording of their conclusion to see what they think.

It's worth stressing again that a *cum hoc* or a *post hoc* argument is not necessarily flawed. In this case, for example, it could be that TV-watching in itself does increase blood pressure in children (by reducing the metabolic rate more than just sitting reading, talking, drawing, and so on).

GENERALISATIONS

As we're seeing time and time again, with any evaluation, we must always look very carefully at what the author has done with their inference. The wording of the claim(s) and the inference(s) are crucial here. The more the inference goes further than the claim allows, the more of a problem we've got. Using our bank account model, we either need more in the claim or less in the inference.

Look at the next example:

> In a study at Oxford University, crows used a long stick to get at some food that was placed out of their reach at the end of a transparent tube. This was the first time that using tools in complex sequences had been seen in non-human animals. It shows that a wide range of birds and other animals have abilities in logical thinking, planning and creativity way beyond what we would expect.

Is this an argument in which the conclusion can straightforwardly be drawn from the evidence-claims? What's going on?

The author goes from evidence about the crows used in the Oxford study to 'a wide range of birds and other animals'. Is this acceptable? As you will have seen, the author accepts the move from these crows by assuming that they are representative of this wide range of other animals. This assumption focuses us on the issue here. We might want to ask some questions.

- Are these crows typical of other crows?

- Are crows typical of other birds?

- Are these crows typical of a 'wide range of birds and other animals'?

The author obviously thinks that the answer to each of the questions is 'yes'. But the jump from these crows could be a problem. What we have is an example of *generalisation*. The author takes these crows as typical not only of other crows but of many other species. This might or might not be OK. Given that we didn't realise before that crows could do what these crows did, we might well be underestimating how non-human animals can solve problems.

Using our bank balance method, to reduce the range of the generalisation, we would need to reduce what the inference takes out.

> In a study at Oxford University, crows used a long stick to get at some food that was placed out of their reach at the end of a transparent tube. This was the first time that using tools in complex sequences had been seen in non-human animals. It shows that crows have abilities in logical thinking, planning and creativity way beyond what we would expect.

In this version, all we have to do is to make the first assumption on our list. Even though there still might be an issue here of whether these Oxford crows are typical of all crows, it doesn't seem unreasonable to think that they are. So this seems much less overdrawn. (Of course, a visiting alien conducting research on some people in Oxford might make a mistake in generalising their thinking abilities to all humans. But perhaps not.)

This issue of generalisation is an interesting one. Too often we find it included in Critical Thinking books as an example of a weakness in argument. But the authors of such books don't think about generalisation properly.

We generalise all the time without making serious errors of judgement. We infer from the fact that traffic went round a certain way on roundabouts yesterday that it will do so today. We infer that cooking potatoes will soften them today just like it has done every other time. Of course, the predictability involved in these generalisations is not a problem. But, when predictability is less secure, how far can we generalise from evidence about some examples of X to all cases of X?

So when you read or are told that generalisation is a weakness in argument, ignore it. It is not generalisation as such that is the problem, but *over-generalisation*: in other words, when the evidence-claim hasn't got enough in it to take us as far as the inference that's drawn. This can work both ways. A single example of X is not normally enough to draw an inference about lots of Xs. And it's a problem the other way round too: evidence of lots of Xs isn't necessarily a reliable guide to a single example of X.

Our example of the creative crows above highlighted the need to look at the relationship between the evidence and the inference from it. We felt able to generalise from these crows to all crows, in that the ones used were presumably not pre-selected for their creativity. But whether we could actually generalise to every single crow around might be more problematic. (Perhaps, like people, some are less creative than others.)

Look at the following description of the US swimmer Michael Phelps, the winner of 16 Olympic gold medals:

> Phelps has a 6ft 7in armspan and the flexibility of a limbo dancer. He is tall at 6ft 4in but he is almost all back, with comparatively short legs and two huge feet. (*The Times*, 18 August 2009)

Here we have someone who presents problems of generalisation. In an obvious way, we would not expect to be able to generalise from Michael Phelps to the vast majority of swimmers. As Professor Whyte, an expert in sport science, has said about him, 'people aren't made to move like that'. But there is a way that Phelps could be used for generalisation. Professor Whyte has done this by stressing that those who will push sporting performance forward will be like Phelps, people who are different in all sorts of physical ways.

So Michael Phelps illustrates the point that generalisation is always something to be considered in relation to what's actually going on. What inference is being drawn from what claim?

Incidentally, you'll sometimes see over-generalisation given as 'hasty generalisation'. This is a strange version. There is nothing essentially hasty about over-generalising. Someone could take all day to do it. Even if 'hasty' means something like 'not giving enough thought to it', it's a problem. Someone could think a lot about it and then still over-generalise. So it's best to stick with the latter term: it accurately expresses what's going on.

So far, we've looked at two problems with arguments: seeing correlation as essentially causation, and over-generalisation. These are both examples of weakness in argument as a result of inadequate evidence. You can see why. The problem with troubling *post hoc* and *cum hoc* arguments is that the evidence is not enough for the author to draw their conclusion. As we saw, there could be alternative (and acceptable) explanations for the correlation. In the same way, the problem with over-generalisation is that the evidence isn't enough: the author has given it more significance than it's likely to have.

SLIPPERY SLOPE ARGUMENTS

There is another type of argument whose weakness is due to inadequate evidence. It's illustrated in the following example:

In August 2008, the sociologist Dr Jessica Ringrose wrote an article in which she argued that teenage girls should be taught more about positive female role models such as Emmeline Pankhurst (and the admirable Lisa Simpson). This argument enraged one contributor to the *Daily Mail*.

> Students need to be educated properly, not taught political nonsense! I guess (people like this) want girls taught anti-male propaganda, and will push for lessons on how to kill their future husbands, should they so choose!

At the very least we would say that the response seems very much over the top. Dr Ringrose had argued that the purpose of teaching girls about positive role models was to stop the trend of girls describing themselves as 'slut' and 'whore' – abusive terms normally used by males. For our contributor from Bolton (in the UK), this is seen as 'anti-male propaganda'. But this isn't the real problem (weird though it is). It's what comes next that's really troubling for a Critical Thinker. Why does teaching girls about positive role models lead to 'lessons on how to kill their future husbands'?

Though the man from Bolton hasn't produced an argument as such, what he has done is to give us an example of another form of weakness in which the evidence is inadequate. This is called a *slippery slope* argument. It should be pretty clear why. Our man from Bolton sees that going down the line of teaching girls about positive role models so that they don't refer to each other as 'slut' or 'whore' takes us down a slippery slope to lessons on murdering husbands. It's a slippery slope because it takes us from *x* to a very distant *y* with no obvious connecting points in the argument. It's as if, as he presents it, once you accept *x*, then you're committed to *y*. And this is a familiar usage of the slippery slope argument. Someone is pointing out (very often wrongly) that, if you accept or argue for something, then all sorts of ghastly consequences will follow (without explaining why). You can also see why slippery slope is sometimes described as the 'thin end of the wedge'.

The reason that a slippery slope argument is an example of inadequate evidence is that, as with the other types, the initial starting point for the argument isn't enough to justify where it ends up. This is a very important point. If it could be shown that the starting point *was* enough to justify the conclusion, then we don't have a slippery slope: we have instead an acceptable argument showing why if A, then B; if B, then C; if C, then D...if P, then Q; therefore, if A, then Q. In this sort of argument, each move needs to work, needs to follow. If it does, then we can travel a long way from the starting to the end point of the argument.

> Our wish for convenience and safety ends up killing Arctic animals such as polar bears and sea lions. So, for the sake of Arctic animals, we should live with less convenience and safety.

This argument looks odd. The connections between convenience, safety, and the death of polar bears and sea lions are not made. It has the look of a weird slippery slope. So what's going on?

> There are many chemicals that are widely used to make things more convenient and safe for us. For example, we insist on having non-stick saucepans. But, to get those, we need to use the chemical called PFOS. In addition, to make our clothing and furniture safer, we use flame-retardant chemicals called PBDEs. Poor regulation of these chemicals means that they end up in the water supply and thus, by sea and ocean currents, reach the Arctic. They also drift there in air currents. The fish in the Arctic Ocean become contaminated by PFOS and PBDEs. Polar bears and sea lions (and seals) eat the fish, thus becoming contaminated themselves. Such animals also take in the pollution by breathing in the contaminated Arctic air. In this way, our wish for convenience and safety ends up killing polar bears, sea lions, seals, and other animals such as whales, walruses, and reindeer. So, for the sake of Arctic animals, we should live with less convenience and safety.

You can see that, in this developed form, the move from saucepans and sofas to the death of polar bears is well-developed in a very relevant explanatory way. Though the move is a big one, it is not a slippery slope. All the connections are added, and the connections seem to be acceptable.

The very term slippery slope always suggests something negative (as does thin end of the wedge). But sometimes we can reverse this. Sometimes the move from A to Q takes us somewhere good. It's what I call a controlled climb.

> If supermarkets can have lots of GM food (like tomatoes) on their shelves, then we'll end up saving thousands of endangered creatures, like orang-utans. So we should encourage supermarkets to stock lots of them.

So how have we gone from GM foods on supermarket shelves to orang-utans?

(sequence 1) GM foods → fewer pesticides → more insects surviving → more animals feeding on insects survive

+ (sequence 2) GM foods → bigger crops → less land needed for cultivation → less cutting down of forests and other destruction of animal habitats

(sequence 1) + (sequence 2) → thousands of endangered species survive

Though there might be disagreement with the content of the argument, the end-product of the sequence is something straightforwardly good.

You might have seen that when someone is accused of leading us down a slippery slope, there's something about consistency going on. What's being said is that, if you believe / argue for / accept / want x, then, to be consistent, you must accept what comes with / follows x. In that the slippery slope isn't normally spelled out, this consistency is often left vague. For example, the attack on Dr Ringrose that educating girls about positive female role models leads to females murdering their husbands isn't obviously a consistency issue. To see how it might be, perhaps we should seek to get into the head of the man from Bolton. Here we go:

If you think girls should be taught positive female role models, then you must think that they should be taught to see men in a negative light, so you must think that girls should be given the skills to deal with the negative aspects of males, so you must think that they shouldn't have to put up with the negative features of males, so you must think that they can kill men.

That was a very slippery slope. Let's get out of here.

We'll meet the issue of consistency again later in this chapter.

STRAW MAN ARGUMENTS

We've so far looked at types of argument in which weakness comes from the use of inadequate evidence. There is another category of weak arguments. These are those which have irrelevant evidence. Though irrelevant evidence is in an important way inadequate, there is some value in making the distinction.

Whereas inadequate evidence could possibly by supplemented or developed by adding in some extra evidence of the same type, irrelevant evidence just stops us in our tracks. Even if we added some more of the same type, it's just more irrelevance. The first example of this category of weak arguments takes us to meet a weak and vulnerable man.

In Chapter 5 we looked at how counter-arguments are sometimes included by an author in order to knock them down. This is fine although, of course, the author might not knock it down effectively. But there is another point that needs considering. We have to take it that the counter-argument is being presented accurately (or perhaps, more to the point, fairly).

We'll look at this by using an example from *The Times*. After concerns about possibly over-aggressive policing in dealing with demonstrations in summer 2009 in the UK, there was some correspondence in this newspaper about what the police should be allowed to do. Here's someone's contribution from 8 August:

> Here's an idea: let's take away the officers' extending batons, shields, stab vests, helmets, CS spray and handcuffs and just have them all politely inform wrongdoers and criminals to be nice. Because that would work wouldn't it?

The force of this position (it's not technically an argument, as you can see) is that the criticism of the police methods is unjustified. And it's not justified, our *Times* reader thinks, because the alternative is ridiculous.

Hopefully, you'll be able to see at least one problem with what's going on here. The problem that perhaps hits us first is that the counter-position seems ludicrous. Nobody, presumably, would say that the police should 'politely inform wrongdoers and criminals to be nice'. And this problem is a serious one. If someone distorts the counter-position, then any argument against it is pretty meaningless. This is because it's then a pointless argument.

This distortion of the counter-position has a name. It takes its name from what's going on here. Why would someone distort a counter-position? Presumably because the distortion makes it easier to attack it. If the counter-position is presented in a deliberately weak version, then it should be easier to show how weak it is, to knock it down. So the name of this type of arguing is *straw man*. A straw man isn't a real man; a straw man is a weak version of man; a straw man can be easily knocked down, can be blown away.

The straw man argument can be seen in terms of irrelevant evidence because what the author presents as the claim made by the other side is irrelevant. They're saying something that isn't the case.

Here's another straw man argument. Interestingly, it's also on the topic of law and order. Indeed, this is often where you'll find them. People can easily find chaos lurking around every corner. The next person (*The Times* letters page, September 2009) worries that not locking up criminals for life is a problem. Their letter followed the suggestion that Scouts and Guides are no longer to be allowed to carry their traditional sheath knives.

> Are we now going to stop people buying climbing ropes; are we going to take the kukri [a curved knife] away from the Gurkha soldier? What if the Brigade of Guards takes exception to the Secretary of State for Defence during Trooping of the Colour? (Rubber bayonets?) We need to make punishment mean punishment...

You will see that, when a straw man argument is used, the arguer is showing the position they're attacking as an absurd one. This technique of showing a position as absurd also has a name, a Latin name: *reductio ad absurdum* – reduction to absurdity. This person is saying that the solution to knife crime is not to ban knives but to lock up for life those people who use them criminally. They defend their position by reducing the opposing position to absurdity – if you ban knives, then you have to ban rope (in case someone uses it to strangle you?), and you have to ban the Gurkhas from using their knives, and the Brigade of Guards have to use rubber bayonets. Clearly all of these are absurd, and their absurdity shows the straw man because, as we've seen, nobody is saying that *all* knives have to be banned.

RESTRICTION OF OPTIONS

We'll leave straw men blowing in the wind (having seen that, despite what Bob Dylan might say, they're not the answer). But, having left them behind, let's have another look at the first straw man argument:

> Here's an idea: let's take away the officers' extending batons, shields, stab vests, helmets, CS spray and handcuffs and just have them all politely inform wrongdoers and criminals to be nice. Because that would work wouldn't it?

There's something else worth noting about it. There's another weakness. This is that the issue of policing demonstrations is reduced to two possibilities: to allow the police to carry on as before or to get them to speak politely to criminals. Those are the only possibilities allowed. It could be that there are other possibilities: using different policing methods or allowing demonstrations to take place only within a limited area are two of them.

Here we have yet another weakness of inadequate evidence. The author is claiming that there are two positions to consider. There are others, so their presentation of the evidence is inadequate. This weakness is called (not surprisingly) *restriction of options*. It's also sometimes called *false dilemma*.

It's important to note that restriction of options is a problem only when there are more options than the ones presented by the author. This means that sometimes there really will be only two options; it also means that sometimes there will be more than three, four, five, and so on.

> The Nazi war criminal, Aribert Heim, is either still alive or is now dead. We have no firm evidence that Heim is dead, so we should proceed to look for him on the basis that he is still alive.

In this example, it is true that Heim is either alive or dead. These two options exhaust the range of possibilities. So there is no inappropriate restriction of options here.

> The Second World War began with the invasion of Poland by Germany on 1 September 1939. Things might have been very different, however, if Russia hadn't agreed a prior secret pact with Germany, carving up Poland between them. The invasion might have been postponed or might never have taken place. Stalin's willingness to do business with Hitler almost certainly contributed to Hitler's decision to invade Poland at this time.

In this example, two options are given. The invasion of Poland might have been postponed or not have taken place. There is, however, an obvious third possibility that it might have gone ahead anyway (given Hitler's determination to expand German territory). You might want to consider a fourth possibility that the invasion would have taken place earlier but this doesn't seem to fit well with the point about the agreement with Russia.

In this last example, then, there is an inappropriate restriction of options. You will recall that the other term that we used was 'false dilemma'. A dilemma is normally taken to be a situation in which someone is faced with two choices, each of which creates problems. Let's have a look at a problem someone's faced with, having had a good meal served to them by a pleasant and efficient waiter or waitress.

> Should I leave a tip? The service was very good, so it would be appropriate to reward the staff. But I've got a problem with that. If I (and people like me) leave a tip, that will allow the system to continue by which staff are paid very badly because the management knows that diners leave tips. But, if I (and people like me) don't, the waiting staff will have to live on low wages even though they've done a really good job. So...?

A real problem indeed but is it technically a dilemma? Is there at least one other thing that could be done? Perhaps our diner could start a campaign to increase the low wages of catering staff. They could, but it doesn't solve the immediate problem. They could leave a very small tip, but that's contained within the first option. So our diner needs to resolve what amounts to a dilemma one way or another before they leave the restaurant.

CIRCULAR ARGUMENTS

Whilst our diner puzzles over whether to leave a tip, we'll head off to look at other examples of problematic arguments. Having just considered a problem of inadequate evidence, here's another one. This is a strange one. Have a look at the next example:

> Showing the dangers of drinking alcohol to young people can make drinking it look attractively risky. Therefore making alcohol-drinking look dangerous can have the effect of making it look appealing by being risky.

The oddity of this argument will probably have slapped you in the face. Arguments are supposed to go somewhere. The significance of the → in the process of claim → inference (or R →C) is that there is some movement. The inference is *drawn* from the claim. In the example above, the inference is the *same as* the claim: there is no movement. The first claim is equivalent to the second.

This is the most extreme form of inadequate evidence, in that there isn't any. This form of argument is called *circular*, for obvious reasons. It's also sometimes referred to as 'begging the question'. More often than not, however, you'll see this second term used wrongly. It's normally used in the wrong sense to mean 'this raises the question'. You'll find that politicians often use it like this.

Vincent Cable of the Liberal Democrats responded to the Government's plan to save money by making public services more efficient by saying, 'This begs the question why, if efficiency could be improved, wasn't it done earlier?'

Though there is debate as to the exact way in which the term 'begging the question' should be used, this is not one of them. There is a perfectly good alternative which is 'raising the question'. So Vincent Cable should have said 'This raises the question why...'

Circular arguments are always a problem because you can't infer something without having given at least one reason for it.

Before we leave these arguments, let's just check back to an argument that we took to be a valid argument.

No vegetarians eat meat.

Martha Phillips is a vegetarian.

So Martha Phillips doesn't eat meat.

Perhaps you're thinking that this is a form of question-begging, in that the conclusion, as we saw, is contained in the reasons. But the conclusion is not equivalent to either reason, unlike in our dangers of drinking example earlier in which the conclusion was no more than a restatement of what had been already claimed.

AD HOMINEM ARGUMENTS

Having gone round in circles, we're off to look at another weakness in argument. This time it's another one involving irrelevant evidence. Here's an example. It refers to the controversy in September 2009 about the Tate Modern's decision to show, as part of the exhibition 'Pop Life', a photograph of a naked Brooke Shields taken when she was 10.

Amongst the contributors to the online comments section of the *Daily Mail* website on September 30 was this one, from Steve from Wiltshire.

(As) a father of young girls I am disgusted that such exhibits are permitted. It's part of the same sick liberal conspiracy to undermine decency. Bearded, sandal-wearing, muesli-eating, liberal *Guardian* readers will no doubt find it acceptable.

Steve might well be disgusted that the Brooke Shields photograph is being exhibited, but he has not given any well-formulated reason why it shouldn't be, beyond his disgust. And you can see that the argument starts to look very thin if we use just this:

> Steve from Wiltshire is disgusted that a photograph of a naked 10-year-old Brooke Shields is being exhibited at the Tate Modern. Therefore it shouldn't be exhibited.

If we add in some of his other observations, then does it become stronger?

> Steve from Wiltshire is disgusted that a photograph of a naked Brooke Shields is being exhibited at the Tate Modern. Bearded, sandal-wearing, muesli-eating, liberal *Guardian* readers will no doubt find it acceptable. Therefore it shouldn't be exhibited.

As you can see, the argument has become very strange indeed. The second reason does nothing. Even if it were the case that bearded people who wore sandals (Socrates, Moses, Jesus, and so on), who eat muesli (perhaps you), who read the *Guardian* (about 1.3 million) did find it acceptable, this is not a reason not to exhibit the photograph. In fact, it has probably occurred to you that Steve's argument seems to backfire because there seems to be rather a lot more people wanting to allow it than Steve wanting it not to be shown.

What you will have seen is that Steve's position relies on using irrelevant features of people (beards, sandals, breakfast choice, newspaper choice) rather than useful reasoning. But, you might want to point out, there's still something else that he said (the second sentence). So let's put that into the argument:

> Steve from Wiltshire is disgusted that a photograph of a naked Brooke Shields is being exhibited at the Tate Modern. Bearded, sandal-wearing, muesli-eating, liberal *Guardian* readers will no doubt find it acceptable. Such people are part of the same sick liberal conspiracy to undermine decency. Therefore it shouldn't be exhibited.

We've now got something a little stronger. But only if we repackage it.

Steve from Wiltshire is disgusted that a photograph of a naked Brooke Shields is being exhibited at the Tate Modern. People who want it exhibited are conspiring to undermine decency. Therefore it shouldn't be exhibited.

The first reason ('Steve from Wiltshire...') still lacks any useful strength in the argument. The second reason (the repackaged one) might have some strength but only if it is indeed the case that the people who want the picture shown are indeed 'conspiring to undermine decency' (whatever is meant by 'conspiring' and 'decency'). And only if the assumption is added that 'showing this picture of Brooke Shields will undermine decency'. And only if others are added: 'undermining decency is a bad thing'; 'there is agreement on what is decency'; 'the photograph of Brooke Shields isn't tasteful/beautiful/...'

So it turns out to be a very weak argument. But to push this point home, let's just refocus on Steve's third sentence. This is the attack on those who might wish the picture to be shown, given in terms of personal characteristics. The point is that it is utterly irrelevant to this argument whether someone has a beard, wears sandals, eats muesli, or reads the *Guardian*. This description is meant to be abusive (and thus powerful). But, unfortunately for Steve, the abuse weakens the argument considerably.

What we have in this example is a type of weakness with another Latin name – *ad hominem*. This literally means 'to or at the man'. What this refers to is that the arguer is arguing against something, by attacking the *source* of that argument rather than the argument itself (so you'll sometimes see it as 'attacking the arguer rather than the argument'). This is what makes the attack irrelevant. Even if the people who argued for the showing of the photograph were bearded and wore sandals as they chewed their muesli whilst reading the *Guardian*, these would be irrelevant things in the argument as to whether or not the photograph should be shown.

We'll now look at another form of weakness through irrelevant evidence. It comes in different forms. In one form, it's related to *ad hominem*. This is because it refers to arguments in which the arguer attacks features of those on the other side.

TU QUOQUE ARGUMENTS

The next example is taken from an article about the demonstration in London about the G20 summit in April 2009. This part of the article refers to the presence at the demonstration of Russell Brand, the comedian who earlier in the year had been sacked by the BBC.

> Outside the Bank of England, Brand told the demonstrators he was angered by the 'financial disparity' in the world. This after spending the last few months, since he was run out of the BBC, flying round the world – coining it in Hollywood, playing to packed houses on a sell-out tour of Australia and luxuriating on a five-star holiday in Malawi. (*Daily Mail*, 3 April 2009)

Though there are straightforwardly abusive remarks made about Brand elsewhere in the article (such as 'Brand epitomises a generation of self-obsessed exhibitionists'), this particular approach is doing something different. It is using inconsistency as an issue in order to attack Brand. It is saying that here we have Brand demonstrating against 'financial disparity' (the rich stay rich and the poor stay poor, presumably) whilst at the same time enjoying an expensive life of Riley, available only to the rich.

So is this a position which has any strength? In some ways it has. It is, in effect, saying something like 'you claim to believe in/support *x*, but you also want to do/support the opposite of *x*'. In this way, the author is seeking to discredit the argument of someone who acts inconsistently. This works at one level. We have already stressed that inconsistency in an argument is a very big problem. But what we have to remember is that the argument that someone is trying to discredit isn't itself discredited as a result of this particular type of inconsistency.

This way of arguing gives us another Latin name – *tu quoque* (pronounced 'tyou kwokway'). This simply means 'you too'. In the passage above, the author is saying that Russell Brand is just as guilty of the things he's protesting about. He lives the life of a rich person, even though he condemns the fact that such a life is possible only for a small minority. But, as we've seen, there's a distinction between a *tu quoque* argument like this and one that attacks the argument that's being presented. Thus, in the Russell Brand example, the author might have a point that there is an inconsistency between Brand's apparent concern for the rich to be less rich and his own rich lifestyle.

There is, however, another version of *tu quoque*. This is the one more commonly identified as *tu quoque* and, though there is a difference between this version and the first one, this second one is also concerned with the problem of consistency. The next example should show what's going on.

The sprinter Ben Johnson won the gold medal in the 100 metres at the 1988 Olympics. However, he was stripped of this medal when it was found that he had been using banned performance-enhancing drugs. Following an enquiry into the use of such drugs in athletics (which showed that he wasn't the only athlete to have taken such drugs), Johnson commented to the *Toronto Star* that 'It was (for years) like I was the only cheat. I knew time would take care of the truth.' Clearly the revelations that drug use was widespread amongst many athletes have shown that Johnson was harshly treated.

In this argument, Ben Johnson's cheating is seen as less serious than it had been, on the grounds that he was not the only cheat. This type of argument is based on the point that something apparently unacceptable that's been done or defended is acceptable on the basis that the same thing is done or defended by others. You can see how the term 'you too' fits here. It's someone saying, 'That person might have behaved badly, but so have others, so what he's done isn't so bad.' You can also think of this in terms of 'two wrongs don't make a right'.

The weakness of this type of argument can be highlighted in all sorts of situations. Here's an interesting historical example:

The film *The Gathering Storm* (2002) was about Winston Churchill and his concern about the prospect of war with Germany. There is a scene in it when a German diplomat is asked by a British civil servant, 'Is it true that you have built a concentration camp outside Munich to incarcerate Jews and other enemies of the Reich? Or is that...propaganda?'

The German replies, 'But it was you British who invented the concentration camp, to detain your enemies the Boers during the South African War.'

Apart from the fact that it was the Spanish who 'invented' the concentration camp when they imprisoned Cuban rebels, here we have a good example of someone not responding to a point as such. They merely accuse the questioner of being the same. In this case, just because the British once used what could be called 'concentration camps' doesn't mean that the Germans weren't using them. In examples like this, 'you too' arguments get us nowhere (which is, of course, the intention).

Another example is the use of the accusation of *tu quoque* by those people who are opposed to the use of the death penalty in the US. Part of their argument is that, if the State sees murder as a very serious crime, then how can it justify killing people by executing them? Clearly here we have a point about definition: is 'murder' the same as 'execution'? But the issue of consistency is certainly there, and the charge of *tu quoque* is worth examining in this example.

We have looked at many examples of weakness of argumentation, some stemming from irrelevant evidence and others from inadequate evidence. In the rest of this chapter, we're going to look at special types of weakness, which again are examples of irrelevant evidence.

APPEALS

There is a group of types of argument that uses what are termed 'appeals'. As with any sort of claim, an appeal needs to be judged in terms of whether or not it's relevant.

So what do we mean by 'appeals' in Critical Thinking? They are a category of claims in which some feature or quality is used to try to argue a particular point. We'll start with the appeal to popularity.

APPEALS TO POPULARITY

In a survey carried out in 2009, it was found that 51 per cent of the British population believe that evolution is not enough to explain the development of the structure of living things. So we must seriously doubt the role of evolution, as described by Charles Darwin.

This argument uses the evidence of public belief about evolution to argue that we must doubt evolution. It uses no other evidence. So is the evidence relevant? Straightforwardly, absolutely no. Darwin's account of evolution as the explanation for the development of species cannot be judged by what the public thinks of it. It either works as a scientific explanation or it doesn't. It would be like condemning the view that the Earth moves around the Sun on the grounds that, five hundred years ago, the widespread view was that the Sun moved around the Earth.

Public back view that Earth is the centre of the universe. (The Papal Mail, 10 June 1585)

With the argument about evolution, we have an irrelevant appeal to popularity. It uses irrelevant evidence, so it is a very weak argument. So what does a relevant appeal to popularity look like? Is it like this one?

50 per cent of the US population believe that we should keep troops in Afghanistan, with 43 per cent opposed to this. Because there is still a majority in favour of having troops there, the US should continue to do so.

Public opinion surveys are often quoted to show what ought or ought not to be done. But are they relevant appeals to popularity? In this previous example (from September 2009), the figures are fairly close, but the bigger number is in favour of US troops fighting in Afghanistan. Does it follow therefore that the US should keep troops there?

This is a more difficult one. In that governments in democratic countries are supposed to take some notice of public opinion (if nothing else, so that they can win elections), then this evidence is not irrelevant. But it could be said that it is only weak evidence. Perhaps the public have insufficient information or understanding of the issues involved. Perhaps, therefore, an appeal to popularity on a number of issues needs, at best, to be only part of the evidence.

Any argument which wants to infer the *truth* of something, where the truth is something unaffected by what the wider public thinks, is going to have an irrelevant appeal to popularity. As we have seen, examples here include evolution (the truth of which is unaffected by public opinion). Another subject is GM foods. Even if the majority of the public is against their widespread use, this isn't relevant to whether or not they're a partial solution to solving food shortages.

Arguments which are concerned with how public opinion (or part of it) might affect what *ought* to be done *might* have relevant appeals to popularity. Thus we could make a distinction between an argument looking at whether or not capital punishment deters people from crime and an argument looking at whether it is acceptable to execute people. In the first argument, public opinion will not tell us whether or not capital punishment works as a deterrent; in the second, acceptability can (although doesn't need to) be based on what the public thinks.

APPEALS TO PITY

We'll now move on to another type of appeal. You are likely to have seen some of the reality TV programmes, in which people (normally unknown members of the public) audition and then, if initially acceptable, perform as part of a process which can lead to fame and riches. The defining characteristic is meant to be talent. In the programme called *X-Factor* (in the UK), the relevant talent is the ability to sing. So, if the programme works, the contestant with the greatest ability to sing should win. However, an appeal to popularity is built into the selection process, which raises a problem straightaway. But there is more. Talent might, at times, be sacrificed for something else. This is *pity*. Just listen while some young man or woman warbles on, with the obligatory tears in their eyes.

> I've got to win this, because my Dad died when I was only ten, and my Mum struggled to bring me and my six brothers and sisters up. I just want them to be proud of me, and I want to be able to buy my Mum a nice house, because she's been really ill recently and...

We'll switch them off there. You will have got the point by now. None of this information is relevant to the inference 'I've got to win this', because none of the evidence that follows is anything to do with talent.

What we have here is not an appeal to popularity, but an appeal to pity. And it's an irrelevant appeal to pity. People should win talent shows because they are the most talented, not because they are to be the most pitied. Thus we have here an irrelevant appeal to pity. But, as with appeals to popularity, are there any relevant appeals to pity?

> Bullfighting should be banned as soon as possible. This is called a 'sport' but it is a bizarre sport which allows a bull to be harassed and attacked with spears, swords, and knives. These weapons are inserted into the shoulders of the bull, causing intense pain and thus huge distress. The bull, losing strength from massive blood loss from its injuries, can take up to 20 minutes to die.

Does this work? The conclusion that bullfighting should be banned is drawn from evidence that focuses on the suffering that bulls have to endure in the ring. The intention of the author is that one should feel distress at reading this evidence, distress that is designed to make one pity the bull and thus support the conclusion. It works for me, and it might work for you. If it doesn't, then this will be because you will see what happens to the bull as acceptable. Whether or not it works, this could be seen as a relevant appeal to pity in that it is concerned with what actually goes on in the bullring.

Whilst we're thinking about bullfighting, what do you think of the next piece of information?

In a 2007 survey, 72 per cent of Spanish people said that they had no interest in bullfighting.

If this was used in the above argument, would it be a relevant or an irrelevant appeal to popularity?

You could argue that it looks pretty relevant. If the majority of the Spanish population has no interest, then this would seem to emphasise the lack of justification for the cruelty involved. (Although this is a difficult area: one could not say that the cruelty was less if the majority approved of bullfighting. Pain is pain, regardless of numbers.)

APPEALS TO AUTHORITY

There is another type of appeal that we can bring in here. Here's the British actor and comedian Ricky Gervais on the subject of bullfighting.

What is the pleasure of seeing an animal speared to death? Bullfighting needs to stop – it's so cruel.

We could incorporate this comment into the argument as something like 'the well-known actor and comedian Ricky Gervais says that bullfighting is very cruel and there cannot be any pleasure in watching an animal being speared to death'.

In a way, it provides another line of reasoning. We've had the evidence of cruelty; we've had the lack of interest; we've now got somebody famous emphasising the cruelty. Though Ricky Gervais is not an authority or an expert on the subject of bullfighting, there is a way that his fame is being used to make him look authoritative. And there is a category of appeals called 'appeal to authority'. In some ways, it fits here. Ricky Gervais is seen as an important figure, someone who can add weight to a campaign against bullfighting. This is why the World Society for the Protection of Animals (WSPA) includes his comments on their website.

In a very real sense, of course, what Ricky Gervais thinks is neither here nor there. One website claims that Madonna and Celine Dion support bullfighting. Does their apparent support make the case against bullfighting less strong? No.

So, are there appeals to authority which are relevant? This is where we need to slide in another appeal, which sits in the same place. This is 'appeal to expertise'. An appeal to an authority as a relevant expert is something that is different. The appeal isn't to a simply well-known figure, but to someone (or, indeed, an organisation) whose expertise is relevant to the argument.

This would mean that, though Prince Charles often makes his views known on the subject of architecture, we should not see his views as significant in that he has no obvious expertise in this area. (The same point applies to his views on organic and GM foods.)

If we wanted to produce an argument against buying organic food, then we could use the evidence of an expert.

> The Prince of Wales has encouraged people to buy organic food, including his own 'Duchy Originals' brand. However, there is a lot of doubt about the value of organic food. Not only is it more expensive than non-organic food, but the benefits are very difficult to find. In a study published in 2009, a report on organic food by the London School of Hygiene and Tropical Medicine was published. The study was led by Dr Alan Dangour, an expert in public health nutrition. It found that there was no significant benefit from drinking milk or eating meat, vegetables, fruit, and eggs from organic sources when compared with those from non-organic sources. Therefore, people should not buy organic food if they do so in order to have health benefits.

In this argument, the Prince of Wales's position is contrasted with that of a group of experts, the leader of which had expertise in a very relevant subject. In this way, the appeal to expertise is a very relevant one and makes the argument much stronger. Anyone wanting to argue in favour of organic food by appealing to the authority of the Prince of Wales will have a problem showing him to be an expert.

Of course, an appeal to expertise which might work in one area won't necessarily work in another. If we wanted to argue about the state of the Royal finances, then we might wish to appeal to the expertise (and authority) of the Prince of Wales, and leave Dr Dangour to concentrate on looking at the nutritional benefits of non-organic carrots.

Whilst we've got the Prince of Wales away from his pleasant but expensive organic marmalade, he might be interested in another appeal.

APPEALS TO HISTORY

The UK Royal Family provides an important historical role in the country: it provides continuity. Apart from a few years in the middle of the seventeenth century, there has been a monarchy in Britain for over a thousand years. This long-established continuity is something that we shouldn't abandon lightly.

In this example, there is an appeal to history (which can also be seen as an appeal to tradition). You can see how it works: x has been going on for some time, so it should continue. At an important level, it's not a very powerful appeal, if there are reasons to suggest that the tradition or historical continuity are no longer good reasons (perhaps things have changed in relevant ways; perhaps there are now better ways of doing things).

Good examples could be found in sport. The tradition of starting athletic races with the sound of a gun has been shown to be a problem because, in these days of measuring athletic performance in terms of hundredths of a second, there is the problem that those nearest the sound have a very slight advantage (because of the speed at which sound travels). So, to say, 'we've done it like this for a long time' turns out to be a poor reason to continue with the practice. Similarly, an appeal to tradition or history in other sports can be countered with reasons that show the advantages of using new methods. For example, the use of video replays in cricket and the 'Hawk-Eye' electronic system in tennis could be relevant to other sports, such as football.

We've looked at some appeals that are used in argument. It needs to be remembered that appeals are not in themselves weaknesses. You might see that some people lump together 'flaws and appeals' as if appeals are inevitable weaknesses. We have seen that doing this shows a misunderstanding of the nature of appeals. It is only when appeals are not relevant to the argument that we have a weakness, the weakness of irrelevant evidence. Any appeal, of whatever sort, needs to be judged in this way.

Enough of weaknesses: we're now going to look at some specific ways of arguing.

ANALOGIES, HYPOTHESES, DEFINITIONS AND PRINCIPLES

ANALOGIES

In 2006, a UK judge refused to impose an antisocial behaviour order on a man who was growing cannabis at his home. The local council had applied for the order and for possession of the man's council house. The judge threw the case out, making the point that cultivating cannabis is 'no worse than having tomato plants'. He explained that he couldn't see how growing cannabis could ever be seen as a nuisance because, for the neighbours, it's no different to them than if tomato plants had been grown.

The judge's argument is an interesting one. What he does is to use one line of reasoning. This is to say that 'if growing tomatoes is not seen as a nuisance, then neither is growing cannabis'. As you can see, he is not making any judgement of whether or not smoking cannabis (or selling it to others) is acceptable. His comment is only about growing it.

The judge is using what we call an *analogy*. This is a common form of argument. In essence, it amounts to using an evidence-claim. In this example, the judge takes the evidence-claim that tomato-growing is not seen as a nuisance. Because, he argues, this is the case, we can infer from this that growing other things sufficiently similar to tomatoes is acceptable. Since growing cannabis is sufficiently similar, then it is acceptable to grow it.

We could represent the argument as a syllogism.

Growing tomatoes is not a nuisance to neighbours.

> Growing cannabis is the same as growing tomatoes.
>
> Therefore growing cannabis is not a nuisance to neighbours.

As with our previous examination of a syllogism, *if* the reasons are true, then so is the conclusion, making this argument a valid one.

In any evaluation of an analogy, we have to consider the degree of similarity between the two parts. This will be particularly significant when, as in the judge's argument, an argument based only on an analogy stands or falls depending on this degree of similarity.

The organisation Christian Aid ran a campaign in 2009 in which they claimed 'For every excuse not to end poverty, we have 10 bright ideas why we can'. One of these was an analogy. (You should be able to evaluate two of the other 'bright ideas', in the light of what we were doing in the previous section on 'appeals' – 'Over 70% of us think poverty eradication is important', and 'the United Nations Secretary-General has categorically stated that it can happen'.)

The 'bright idea' analogy was 'it's a big task, but no bigger than ending slavery and putting a man on the moon'. Just like the tomatoes and cannabis analogy, the claim here is one of similarity: that the achievement of these two big things shows that we can achieve this other big thing. If we put it into an argument form, we get the following:

> The abolition of slavery was achieved. A man was put on the moon. These two things were both very difficult to achieve. Therefore the abolition of poverty can be achieved.

You will probably see that there's a big assumption needed in this argument. This is that 'the abolition of poverty is no more difficult than was ending slavery and putting a man on the moon'. In any analogy we always have this assumption of sufficient similarity. Without it, the argument cannot work.

So our task is to see if this assumption can be supported. The first problem is that, unfortunately, slavery has not been ended. The Anti-Slavery Society makes the point that, though slavery as we normally think of it was abolished in the nineteenth century, it is still practised in various parts of the world today (including Africa). Though the number of slaves is disputed, depending on the definition used, the estimates put the number at around 3 million upwards.

With regard to putting a man on the moon, this was (as most people would accept) achieved in 1969. However, it might be argued that, though it was very difficult and so a hugely impressive scientific and technological achievement, it was not as difficult as ending poverty. For one thing, it did not depend on the co-operation of the government of every country in the world (which ending poverty would). For another thing, the definition of 'putting a man on the moon' is a straightforward one. The definition of 'poverty' is anything but simple: if poverty is ended, does no one go hungry any more? Do certain diseases disappear? Is all housing at least adequate? And yet another thing: would the ending of poverty require a huge redistribution of wealth away from the rich to the poor both between and within countries? Would people like Roman Abramovich agree? Would the Saudi Royal Family agree?

Our problem, as we have seen, is that ending poverty is certainly a bigger (and less clear-cut) task than putting a man on the moon. In addition, in that slavery hasn't yet been abolished, we can't say whether it *can* be abolished (and thus whether the difficulty-level of its abolition is sufficiently similar to that of ending poverty). As a result, since the analogy (or, more accurately, the analogies) does (do) not work well, the argument falls. (This last point, of course, refers to an argument like the tomatoes and cannabis one in which the analogy is the only reason. If it is only one of at least two, then the argument might still stand.)

We have seen with our fairly detailed analysis that we need to treat analogies in the same way that we treat any other evidence-claim. Is the analogy relevant? Is it sufficient for the argument? To do this, we need to focus on similarities and dissimilarities.

What follows is a detailed look at an analogy, by going through an evaluation step by step. The argument is one used by someone who was head of the UK's Youth Justice Board.

> Locking up children who commit crimes is like building more coal-fired power stations. You create future problems by doing so. Therefore we should lock up far fewer young people than we presently do.

What is the analogy?

This analogy compares the problems that will follow putting children who commit crimes in prison with those that will follow building more coal-fired power stations.

What is its function in the argument?

It provides the only reason for the conclusion that we should lock up far fewer young people than we do.

Does the analogy work?

As we have seen, answering this question involves asking other ones:

What are the significant similarities between the situations?

- Building coal-fired power stations could create future problems in terms of using up resources. Locking up young criminals might create future criminals which will then be a drain on the nation's resources. (Consider the use of the term 'resources'.)

- Building coal-fired power stations provides a short-term benefit as does locking up young criminals (electricity + security) but the trade-off for the future brings possible problems (pollution/resentment +...).

- In each case there are alternatives which might have both short- and long-term advantages, thereby avoiding the disadvantages. (Nuclear power/non-custodial sentences; wind power/fines or...?)

What are the significant differences between the situations?

- Building coal-fired power stations presumably creates future health problems in terms of pollution. Locking up young criminals might create future criminals but these are not necessarily a threat to health as such (possibly more to property). Indeed, the evidence suggests that most young offenders have stopped offending by the time they're 25 anyway.

- Building coal-fired power stations could create future problems in terms of using up scarce resources. Locking up young criminals might create future criminals but these will not be a depletion of non-renewable resources.

- Building coal-fired power stations is not something that can be easily changed in the short-term. Putting young criminals in prison can be supplemented quickly by community programmes.

Are there any other aspects of the analogy that need to be considered?

The two situations are similar (although not in the way the author intends) by both providing benefits. Coal-fired power stations provide electricity, and prisons provide security for the public. Both provide employment. Both provide investment in the future (reformed criminals and industrial etc. progress.) In this way, the support which the analogy gives to the conclusion is lessened.

Which of the two is greater – the similarities or the differences? This is a difficult question to answer and we might disagree. I think that, on balance, the differences are greater but there are very interesting similarities. In that the argument relies only on the analogy, the argument is therefore vulnerable to the charge that there are important differences between the two.

It needs to be remembered that, when someone is using an analogy in an argument, we can't respond by saying 'you can't say that: the two things aren't the same'. Of course, they're not *the same*. If they were the same, there wouldn't be an analogy!

Locking up children who commit crimes is like putting children in prison.

All we have is a circular relationship, not an analogy.

Sometimes you'll come across a different version of using an analogy.

People should expect that some space missions don't succeed. Putting a spacecraft safely on Mars is hard and risky. It's not a trip to Grandma's house. (NASA May 2008)

In this example, we have NASA using what's called a disanalogy. As you can see, this takes the negative form of an analogy: this is not like that, so...

You might like to look at this disanalogy in the same way that we looked at the analogy on children in prisons (comparing the similarities and dissimilarities), but this time looking to see if the dissimilarities outweigh the similarities. However many you find on either side, it's pretty clear that they will. In this example, the disanalogy is part of an argument in which it isn't just a question of an analogy-type reason being used as the reason to draw the conclusion. The argument can be seen in the following way:

(R) Putting a spacecraft safely on Mars is hard and risky.

(IC) It's not a trip to Grandma's house.

(C) People should expect that some space missions don't succeed.

You can see that, in this argument, the disanalogy is not necessary for the argument. If it wasn't there, the conclusion could still be drawn. (You might have spotted the assumption that 'trips to Grandma's house normally succeed'.)

Using analogies is, in an important way, yet another example of the importance of consistency in argument. Someone using an analogy in an argument is saying 'here's one situation in which x is the case; here's another in which x also applies/follows/exists, so we should do the same in both situations'. Any demonstration that the two situations are not sufficiently similar weakens this argument for consistency. (With a disanalogy, of course, the process is the other way round: the more similar the two situations are, the less powerful is the argument for inconsistency.)

HYPOTHESES

We can also see analogous reasoning as an example of a particular type of reasoning. The author is saying 'if this happens in a given situation, then the same thing should happen in the other situation.' This type of reasoning is called *hypothetical reasoning*. However it is expressed, it will have an *if. . . then* form. (It could, for example, be 'were this to be the case, then. . .') We'll now look at such reasoning in more detail.

You will remember that we saw an example of this type of reasoning when we looked at slippery slopes. We saw there that there was a problem with the move from the first 'if' to the final 'then', as shown in the example we looked at.

> If you think girls should be taught positive female role models, then you must think that they should be taught to see men in a negative light . . . so you must think that they can kill men.

This showed that with hypothetical reasoning, the connections do need to be justified (as with the controlled climb). Let's look to see if we can use hypothetical reasoning to go somewhere undesirable but in a justified way, rather than slithering down a slippery slope.

The United Nations (UN) warned in 2009 that the population of the world (6.7 billion) would double in the next 40 years if growth rates don't decline. If the world's population did indeed double by the middle of the century, then there would be massive problems of famine, disease, and frequent conflicts over scarce resources, especially water. It is therefore vitally important to look at ways of slowing the growth of population.

As you can see, there are two hypothetical parts of the argument. The first sentence is the first part, and shows that the form of the hypothetical is sometimes reversed (*x*, if *y*). The second sentence is the second hypothetical. The conclusion is drawn from both of them. You can see that the conclusion is justified all the way. (Of course, this does not mean that there aren't assumed steps in the argument. A crucial one sits between the second reason and the conclusion: 'solutions to food and other shortages will not be found'. For example it could be that scientists will be able to create food crops which need little water.)

You will have seen that hypothetical reasoning, when it extends from one such reason to another, is like a chain, with the links connecting in a necessary way to the conclusion. Not surprisingly, then, they are sometimes called 'chain arguments'. Here's another one on the same subject of the problems of population growth:

The Health and Family Welfare Minister of India, Mr Ghulam Nabi Azad, has called for massive efforts to be made to bring electricity to all of the population of India in order to slow down his country's potentially catastrophic population growth. If electricity is made available to all areas (including rural areas), then both electric light and television could be in all homes. 'If there is electricity in every village,' Mr Azad argues, 'then people will watch TV till late at night and then fall asleep. They won't get a chance to produce children.' Mr Azad claims that '80 per cent of population growth can be reduced through TV.' Therefore bringing electricity to all homes in India will solve the problem of population growth.

You can see the way that the chain is created. We can focus on it by labelling each section:

- If A (electricity in all areas), then B (electric light and TV in all homes).

- If B, then C (people will watch TV until late, then fall asleep).

- If C, then D (people won't get a chance to produce children).

- Therefore, if A, then D.

Though we might want to evaluate the argument (in terms of possible issues with C and D), the chain sequence is clear. In case you spotted the assumption between B and C that 'the TV programmes would be good enough to keep people watching', Mr Azad has got there before you, calling for India's TV channels to provide high-quality programmes.

Having seen hypothetical arguments in action, it is time to enter a cautionary note. Look at the next example:

> Herbal remedies are regarded as less toxic and more natural than drugs prescribed by doctors. But we need to remember that, if herbal remedies work, they must be drugs, and if they are drugs, they must have side-effects. Therefore people need to be told that herbal remedies will have side-effects in the same way as any prescribed drug.

You will have noticed the hypothetical argument-chain in the second sentence. There is no problem with this: if A, then B; if B, then C. What should have followed was if A, then D: if herbal remedies work, then (people need to be told) they will have side-effects. Instead, this link in the chain is missing. The author draws a conclusion which is not in a hypothetical form. Given that the rest of the argument is in this form, this should not be done. Perhaps herbal remedies don't work after all, in which case the conclusion cannot be drawn.

So it is important to remember that reasons that are no more than hypothetical require a hypothetical conclusion.

There's another point to mention. We have seen that hypothetical arguments use a form of 'if... then' reasoning. But this does not mean that every time we see an 'if', we've found some hypothetical reasoning.

> We can't say if the world's population will continue to grow at the present rate. There are too many variables to have to consider. Therefore we must plan for both large and smaller population increases.

You can see that, in this example, the 'if' is not part of a hypothetical, in that there's no 'then' that follows it.

DEFINITIONS

There are times when the 'if...then' form of arguing is used in looking at the meaning and significance of words. Here's an example:

> If we define poverty as the absence of want, then we have a problem. Because we then need to define what we mean by 'want'.

This way of using the hypothetical is often used, as here, to highlight a problem with the way in which terms are used. You can see this particular argument heading off in the same direction as it started.

> ...Because we then need to define what we mean by 'want'. If we take it to mean no more than physical wants such as food, water, and shelter, then there are further problems...

Sometimes we find someone using this hypothetical approach to the meaning of a term to emphasise the significance of the Shakespearian question, 'What's in a name?' In the next example, we find a French proposal to pay classes of students money (up to €10,000 per group), in order to achieve class attendance and performance targets. It was started in October 2009 in some schools in Paris. The scheme was introduced to combat increasing levels of high school dropout. It was criticised for, as one group put it, 'buying' students, and, as another put it, for being 'a perversion of the school mission'.

The head of the greater Paris district where it was being introduced is M. Jean-Michel Blanquer. He defended it in an interesting way:

> If we had called it a scholarship everyone would have been on board.

This raises an important point. 'Scholarships' are seen as a good thing: students get money in recognition of either past or predicted performance. They are a reward for being gifted and/or talented. 'Buying' students is seen as going against what education is meant to be about. You can see how this example shows that the choice of a word can change the nature of an argument.

Usefully for us, M. Blanquer ends with another hypothetical:

> If it doesn't work, we will try something else.

Perhaps like calling the payments 'scholarships'? Interestingly, a scheme in New York which offered up to $1000 per student for passing exams was given the title 'Rewarding Achievement'. This has been seen as successful, and perhaps part of its success is the name itself. One of the people behind the scheme spoke of wanting to 'democratize' success – another good word.

We have seen that the use of a word or term can change the way in which an argument is perceived. In 2009, the people of the UK were promised a 'barbecue summer' by the Met Office (the organisation that forecasts the weather). Though the summer turned out be warmer than average, it was also wetter. But what exactly is a 'barbecue summer'? One where you have more barbecues than average (whatever that is)? Here's another example. It's from James, of Manchester, commenting on the *Daily Mail* website:

> Every other person you meet is a public bureaucrat.

The term 'bureaucrat' is normally a term of abuse. We have in particular the term 'faceless bureaucrats'. Though the term has a neutral meaning – an official in a government department – (unlike 'scrounger' or 'waster' or 'hero'), it is one that is often used to condemn the employment of people who are not in the private sector. (So James's word 'public' is unnecessary: an example of a tautology.) Interestingly, on the same day on the same website, we find Noah, from Bolton (a popular place for contributors!), clarifying the content of the term 'bureaucrat' for people like James from Manchester:

> (These are people) like nurses, primary school teachers, bin men, doctors...

So Critical Thinking requires us to look at how words are used. An argument can depend on a particular meaning of a term (normally assumed, but sometimes explained, and sometimes considered in a hypothetical way).

To see how this can be important, consider how we might define 'cheating'. To help you, here's the start of an argument:

> 'Cheating' can be seen as attempting to achieve something you wouldn't be able to achieve without doing it. But, if this is the definition, then there are lots of everyday things that fall within it...

This discussion of definitions takes us to a small but useful area of Critical Thinking:

looking at what are called necessary and sufficient conditions. There are four permutations here.

Something can be necessary, but not sufficient.

> It is a necessary condition of being able to vote in public elections in the UK that one is aged 18 or over.

With this example, we can see that being aged 18 or over is an essential requirement of being able to vote in parliamentary and local elections. But it is not sufficient. Whether or not they're 18 or over, someone in prison is not allowed to vote. Neither is the monarch. Neither is someone who is not entered on the current Register of Electors.

Something can be sufficient but not necessary.

> If you are the eldest son of the monarch in the UK, then you are heir to the throne.

Being the eldest son of the monarch is enough to make you heir to the throne. But this sufficient condition is not necessary. You could be heir to the throne if your parental monarch had no sons and you are the eldest daughter. If the monarch has no children, then their eldest brother is the heir, and so on.

Something can be both necessary and sufficient.

> With breakfast cereals by Nestlé, only packets that have a green flash across them show that 'they are nothing but whole grain'.

So, without the green flash, they will not be just whole grain. But since packets with the green flash are whole grain, the green flash is both necessary and sufficient to show this.

Another example of a condition being both necessary and sufficient is:

> Having a valid ticket for the UK National Lottery showing all six winning numbers for the relevant week and winning at least a share of the jackpot.

Something can be neither necessary nor sufficient.

Having a degree in law does not guarantee that you can be a solicitor in the UK.

Having a degree in law is neither a sufficient nor a necessary condition for being a solicitor. People can become solicitors with a degree in other subjects, provided they have done an additional course in law. People with a degree in law cannot automatically become solicitors.

Living a long life is neither essential nor a guarantee for achieving greatness.

There are many examples of people having achieved greatness in short lives. Good examples are the amazing Mozart (dead at 35); the sublime John Keats (dead as young as 25); the brilliant Alexander the Great (dead, with an empire sorted, at 32); Jesus (dead at around 33, having changed the world).

Living to a ripe old age might bring all sorts of things but it doesn't have to bring greatness. Annie Butler had been the second-oldest woman in Britain until she died in 2009 aged 112. She might well have brought all sorts of delights to the world, but will not be remembered for achieving 'greatness'.

So why should we fret about looking at necessary and sufficient conditions? Because it can be a very useful way of looking at the significance of some claims.

Child poverty has been particularly high in the UK because of a combination of factors, including a high number of children living with lone parents and the relatively low percentage of lone parents who work. ('What will it take to end child poverty?' The Joseph Rowntree Foundation, 2006)

We've already briefly met the problem of defining poverty (when we were looking at hypothetical reasoning above). Here it is again. What is a necessary condition of a child being seen as being in poverty? (Level of income certainly, but is that all? Is it also to do with the school they attend, the diet that they have, and so on?) What is a sufficient condition? The Joseph Rowntree Foundation takes it as being a child that is in a household in which the income is less than 60 per cent of median income (median income is that of the person/household in the middle of the distribution of income).

Using the necessary and sufficient condition approach can, then, point us to ask useful questions. Try it out with a hefty word like 'democracy'. Here are two widely differing positions:

North Korea has a constitution which is described as 'democratic'. According to the Constitution, it is based on universal suffrage (all of those 17 or over have the vote) and secret ballot.

North Korea is rated the least democratic in the world (187th out of 187) by the Economist Intelligence Unit democracy index. It scores 0.86 out of a possible 10.00, including a score of 0.00 for civil liberties and the same for the electoral system.

So what is a necessary condition of a democracy? (Or, more usefully, what are necessary conditions?) Is there a sufficient condition?

Anyway, you might be interested to know that Sweden is rated the best democracy in the world (or, if you like, the most democratic, with an astonishing score of 9.88, followed by Norway, Iceland, the Netherlands, and Denmark). The UK languishes at 21st, primarily because of the low levels of voting and involvement with political parties (a score for this of 5.00, lower than Iraq's 6.67).

PRINCIPLES

Thinking about 'democracy' takes us nicely on to another feature of some arguments. This is the use of *principles*. We met these briefly in Chapter 1 and you might remember that we described them as general statements of what ought to be done or ought to happen. We saw that 'cheating in sport can never be justified' was an example.

Principles can be used as a reason in an argument; they can also be argued for (being then the conclusion of an argument). They can, like any other claim, be assumed. And this point about being like any other claim is an important one.

They are, at one level, a very significant claim. There's a big difference in significance between saying 'we should treat all people with respect' and 'Eating certain sweets can make Ruby hyperactive'. The first claim has a universal application; the second applies only to Ruby. But beyond this significance, there is the point that both claims can operate equally as a reason in an argument.

We should treat all people with respect. Therefore people convicted of even very serious offences should be respected in the same way as those who have not.

Eating certain sweets can make Ruby hyperactive. Therefore we should ensure that Ruby isn't given these sweets.

Returning to the issue of a ban on cheating as a principle, we can see it being used as a reason in the following argument. It introduces a counter-argument that cheating in sport shouldn't be seen as unacceptable and also looks at a *tu quoque* defence of it. But it rejects this defence and, using the principle as a reason, concludes that we should seek to stop it.

Some people say that we should regard cheating in sport as nothing more than something we have to live with. It's just like everything else. People cheat by not paying their tax, by driving too fast, by using their mobile phone in an exam. But just because people cheat in everyday life doesn't mean that we should put up with it in sport. The number of sports in which cheating is being discovered is growing all the time. There are some that everyone hears about, such as athletics and cycling. But these are because we can prove cheating by testing for various substances such as steroids. There are plenty of examples where you can't find cheats by looking in a test tube. There are footballers diving; there are cricketers deliberating losing a game because there are bets on that they will; there are nods and winks going on in horse racing. Just because cheating goes on in many different forms doesn't make it right. Cheating is always wrong, whatever the sport, whatever the method used, whatever the reason for it. There must be a determined effort to stop it as much as we can.

In the next example, the author argues against the principle, seeking to use a *tu quoque* position that, since cheating goes on in all walks of life, it isn't necessarily wrong in sport.

Though cheating is often seen as wrong, there are many examples in everyday life which show that people don't see it like this. As *The New York Times* put it, 'College students take Ritalin to improve their academic performance. Musicians take beta-blockers to improve their onstage performance. Middle-aged men take Viagra to improve their sexual performance. Shy people take Paxil to improve their social performance. The difference is that if athletes want to get performance-enhancing drugs they go to the black market. If the rest of us want performance-enhancing drugs, we go to our family doctor'. So to say that all these things are wrong is to take up a very odd position. In this way, we can see that cheating, whether in sport or in other contexts, isn't always wrong.

One of the things to remember with principles is that they are very demanding reasons. They don't allow for exceptions (except any mentioned in the principle), whereas other types of claim aren't so exclusive. Perhaps we can show that Ruby's hyperactivity has not got anything to do with eating sweets: perhaps she behaves like this because that's what people expect. (There are all sorts of *post hoc* issues going on here.) But you can't start moving from 'poverty shouldn't ever be tolerated' to 'perhaps we can allow lazy people to be poor because they deserve it'. A principle remains a reason, with potentially massive significance. Thus it allows no contradiction.

In the following argument, the principle is not stated: it is assumed.

> It has been shown very clearly that fish can feel pain in the same way that all other animals can. It is obvious then that fishing of whatever sort cannot be allowed.

The assumed principle is that 'it is wrong to inflict pain on all animals'. This principle sits at the centre of this argument, allowing no exceptions. We can't say 'except for catching fish and then putting them back'. We certainly couldn't say 'except for satisfying our need for Omega-3' (unless we get it from fish that have died from natural causes). The power of a principle in an argument, allowing only for consistency, is clear.

We've reached the lofty heights of principles, and been taken above the clouds. Unfortunately, it's time now to descend. And not just to descend to where we were before, but to go down to a world of possible liars and fraudsters.

9

CREDIBILITY OF EVIDENCE

In all that we have done before, we have taken claims that have been made and we have asked the important questions 'what do they mean?' and 'what is their significance?' In other words, we have taken the claim as a given, as something for us to work with by asking these questions. But there might be times when we need to ask the question 'how believable is this claim?'

The word 'incredible' tends to be used these days to mean 'really good', as in 'this plate of pasta is incredible'. But its original meaning is 'not to be believed'. This is sometimes unpacked, as in 'this witness is not a credible one' or 'this report is not credible'. In both cases, the author is saying that what's being claimed is not believable.

We're going to look at reasons why claims might be either believable or not. We're going to use *criteria* to do this. The word 'criterion' is the singular form; 'criteria' is the plural form. Thus we would say 'here is a criterion we can use' and 'here are criteria we can use'. The word 'criterion' comes from a Greek one for a 'means of judging'.

Before we introduce these criteria, let's just consider when we might want (or need) to use them. If you are faced with a claim made by a scientist that a particular product has health benefits, and a similar claim made in an advert, which is the more believable? If you came up with an answer to this, then you must have been using at least one criterion.

If you answered that the scientist was the more credible, then you've done two things. You've judged that the scientist is believable because they're likely to be reporting honestly and accurately; you've also judged that the advert is less believable because the company advertising its product has reasons not to report honestly and accurately.

So what sort of criteria might you have been using? Let's meet them.

MOTIVE

This is a useful criterion to explain why people and organisations make the claims that they do. Though we often think of it in negative terms (like 'she had a motive to kill her husband'), it simply refers to a reason for doing or saying something. Quite simply, someone might have a strong motive to tell the truth (as well as to lie). So with our scientist, they might have a motive to report information accurately because that's how they perceive their role (and what their organisation would expect them to do). Similarly, the person creating the advert has a motive to use information that shows the product in the best light. The information available might be accurate but there might be a motive to select which is used (and how it is presented).

Within motive, we can find two other criteria.

BIAS

Here we have a criterion which again can go both ways (and even then can be subdivided). Bias refers to leaning in a particular direction. This could be leaning towards telling the truth or the opposite. It could also be accidental or deliberate. Someone might not realise that there is other information available, and so does not include it in their claims and arguments. On the other hand, someone might deliberately ignore or suppress some information in order to present their claims and arguments in a particular way. (We're back to a term we've used before – 'cherry-picking' – a term which emphasises how only the good bits, the cherries, are picked.)

VESTED INTEREST

Here we have another criterion which can go both ways. By 'vested interest' we mean that someone or an organisation has a preference for things to go one way rather than another. But, of course, this could result in the truth being told as well as its being distorted. There might be a benefit in information being presented as accurately as possible, as well as one in its being presented inaccurately. Someone who is accused of a crime they didn't commit has a big vested interest in giving the information that would show that they are innocent. Similarly, someone who is accused of committing a crime they did commit has a big vested interest in not telling the truth. (Unless you happen to be George Washington who, having axed his father's favourite cherry-tree, owned up to this act, explaining that 'I cannot tell a lie'. Fortunately his father was thrilled with his truth-telling son.)

The (now infamous) case of Dr Andrew Wakefield's 'evidence' showing a link between the vaccine against measles, mumps, and rubella (MMR) and autism (and chronic bowel disease) is a good demonstration of how vested interest was seen as weakening the claims made. Dr Wakefield was shown to have received funds from lawyers acting for parents trying to show a causal connection between MMR and autism.

EXPERTISE

This is a criterion which is seen as a very strong one. If someone is an expert, we tend to regard their claims as being more credible than someone who isn't. For example, should we pay much attention to the fact that in an October 2009 survey, 62 per cent of the readers of the *Daily Express* didn't believe that global warming was caused by human activity? These people who thought this were presumably not experts, so we can probably discount them (unless you want to resort to an appeal to popularity). We can contrast our *Daily Express* readers with a report from the Scripps Institution of Oceanography which 'with more than a century of exploration and discovery in global sciences...is the world's pre-eminent centre for ocean and earth research, teaching, and public education'. Dr Tim Barnett and his team from this organisation examined literally millions of pieces of data and concluded that there is now no further doubt that global warming has been caused by human activity.

When we looked at the appeal to expertise, we made the point that an appeal will be stronger if the expert has expertise in the appropriate area. Thus, in this example, Dr Barnett's evidence makes the claim about human activity being the cause of global warming a highly credible one. The beliefs of the *Daily Express* readers appear to bring no expertise to the table.

An important example of how expertise is used to support particular arguments is found in the role of expert witnesses in courts. Examples of these are engineers, forensic scientists, handwriting experts, and doctors. But there can be problems with such expert witnesses. For one thing, juries (and judges) might not be able to understand their evidence fully. It might be highly technical. It might be that juries simply see the expert as knowing best, so their testimony becomes one of the main deciding factors in reaching their verdict. Another problem is that experts might get things wrong! This is especially the case when they move from one area of expertise to another, without any real challenge. A good example was from the evidence (now discredited) by Professor Roy Meadow in an infamous cot death case (infamous because of the miscarriage of justice). Professor Meadow was there to give medical evidence, in his expert role as a paediatrician, but added statistical calculation into it as well. His expertise in statistics, however, was inadequate, resulting in him arguing that the probability of there being two cot deaths in an affluent family was 1 in 73 million, when the real figure is 1 in 77.

So the criterion of expertise in judging credibility might well be a strong one, but we still have to take care when assessing it.

But, of course, expertise needs to sit alongside the other criteria. Someone with expertise might well still be biased. So expertise could still be trumped by another criterion. The next one is a strong candidate.

ABILITY TO PERCEIVE

This is sometimes referred to only as 'ability to see' or 'ability to observe'. Neither of these versions is adequate in that this criterion is not concerned with just seeing or observing (in that it includes hearing, touching, smell and feeling). We can also use the alternative term 'sufficient access', which captures the criterion very well. This is because we are focusing on claims from those who were close enough to something to be able to report on what was going on.

This criterion, of course, has particular relevance when there was something to be able to perceive (or have sufficient access to). For example, after the *Titanic* sank in 1912, the US board of enquiry set up to establish why the ship sank was very keen to have the testimony of survivors. Issues like 'did the *Titanic* break in half before she sank?' were put to the witnesses. However, some said the ship did, others that she didn't. We're very much into sufficient access here: were they able to see what was going on in the darkness and confusion? (Or did vested interest override sufficient access, given that the strength of the ship was supposed to be a central feature of its construction?)

However, the ability to perceive isn't relevant just to specific events. It could also be relevant to having sufficient access to information. Thus the credibility of the above Dr Barnett could be enhanced by the fact that he and his team had examined millions of pieces of data. In this way, Dr Barnett's status becomes even greater than it was before.

Sometimes the ability to observe can produce puzzling evidence. Here's someone reporting in September 2009 that they had seen a 'teardrop-shaped object stationary in the sky for two hours':

> '...we could see that it wasn't a hot air balloon. It was silvery/pearly white, teardrop shape, but no basket on the bottom. The inside was dark grey-black...It wasn't moving...' (examiner.com)

Clearly, this can be seen as evidence that one must consider, but what do we do with it? It needs to be assessed in the same way as any other claim. What is its significance? What explanations are there for it? We could use other criteria to help to assess it. For example, what do we know about the person who made the claim? Do they have a motive in making it?

Sometimes the criterion of ability to perceive/sufficient access can be added to that of expertise. This would normally lead to a claim being strengthened. Unfortunately, sometimes this strengthening produces troubling results.

An expert witness in a 'shaken baby' case made the claim:

> 'I have never seen such injuries.'

The jury is faced here with an expert adding significance to his evidence in this case by saying that, in all of the cases he'd seen, this was the worst. This made his claim one that was difficult to dismiss. But, of course, though he might have been telling the truth, this did not mean that the injuries were caused by the defendant. However, the jury were impressed by the significance of this claim and brought in a guilty verdict. Unfortunately, this was the wrong verdict. The defendant was subsequently shown to be innocent. But it's a good (if worrying) example of how one criterion can add force to another.

Here's another criterion.

NEUTRALITY

A simple way of seeing the significance of this criterion is to look at how the female figure of Justice is often depicted. She has scales to weigh the evidence (which is what we're looking at here) and a sword to dispense justice when necessary. But, in addition, in some versions, crucially she's blindfolded. She is dispensing justice merely according to the balance of the evidence, rather than according to any bias one way or the other.

Neutrality is an important criterion because it's the counter-weight to any distortion in the evidence due to deliberate bias. It's no guarantee against bias, of course, because a neutral source could still be accidentally biased.

A good example of neutrality was the BBC's refusal to carry an appeal by the Disasters Emergency Committee for aid to Gaza in 2009. The Director-General saw this as staying out of the problem of being seen to be taking sides in the dispute between Israel and the Palestinians.

A claim which is made (or supported) by a neutral source can normally be seen as being strengthened by this neutrality.

REPUTATION

This can work in opposite directions. Someone or an organisation can have a good reputation and this can serve to strengthen the credibility of claims they make (or support). But a bad reputation would obviously operate to weaken credibility. It might well be that a source with a good reputation is one that has consistently told the truth (or has been seen to do so), and vice versa.

This criterion could go hand in hand with the previous one. A neutral person or organisation could be seen as having a reputation for honesty and, again, vice versa.

When we looked at expertise, we mentioned the Scripps Institution of Oceanography as one which has considerable expertise. But, of course, because of this expertise, it has a massive reputation. And it would be seen as neutral!

CORROBORATION

It's taken as straightforwardly the case that, if we have one claim supported by another, then the claims strengthen the case for their acceptance. Thus in a court of law, having more than one eye-witness giving the same account is seen as lending very useful weight to that version being accepted. This issue of the power of corroboration works wherever we find it.

Similarly, the lack of corroboration is seen as a potential source of weakness. This is especially so if it is not just that there is this lack, but where there is conflicting evidence. ('The *Titanic* did break in half before she sank.'/'The *Titanic* did not break in half before she sank.')

You can begin to see that using credibility criteria is a bit like playing Top Trumps. A criterion such as expertise will often (perhaps even normally) trump one like vested interest. Someone with sufficient access who has a good reputation and who is neutral might go on to trump expertise. And so on . . .

You can therefore see how the credibility of claims can be seen as strong or weak, according to how the criteria stack up.

For example, what combination could give us very strong reasons to believe the evidence?

> Relevant expertise + ability to perceive + neutrality + good reputation = more credible source

What combination could give us very strong reasons to doubt the evidence?

> Lack of relevant expertise + lack of ability to perceive + bias (including vested interest) + poor reputation = less credible source

Let's now look at an issue we first came across in Chapter 7 when we looked at appeals to expertise. This is the vexed issue of organic food.

> The Food Standards Agency (FSA) commissioned a study of the health and nutritional value of organic as opposed to non-organic food. They asked the London School of Hygiene and Tropical Medicine to carry out this study. The leader of the team was Dr Alan Dangour, an expert in public health nutrition.

> The team looked at 52,000 scientific papers which had been published between January 1958 and February 2008. Only 162 of these papers were seen as relevant, and only 55 of these were seen as of sufficient quality to be useful for the study.

> They concluded in their report of 2009 that there was no significant benefit for health and nutrition from drinking milk, eating meat, vegetables, fruit and eggs from organic sources as opposed to non-organic ones.

The Soil Association says that it is a 'charity campaigning for planet-friendly food and farming. We believe in the connection between soil, food, the health of people and the health of the planet'.

The review by the Food Standards Agency, it claims, looked only at papers written in English, and ignored recent research carried out by the European Union which was completed in April 2008. This involved 31 research and university institutes and the publication of over 100 scientific papers. This research showed that 'levels of a range of nutritionally desirable compounds were shown to be higher in organic crops' and that 'levels of nutritionally undesirable compounds were shown to be lower in organic crops'.

So what do we do with these competing claims?

Let's apply the credibility criteria to them and see what happens.

Let's look for neutrality first – it's always a very important criterion.

We perhaps need to know something about the Food Standards Agency. Is it neutral in all of this? (Or is it a front for the non-organic farmers' lobby?) This is what they say about themselves:

The Food Standards Agency is an independent Government department set up by an Act of Parliament in 2000 to protect the public's health and consumer interests in relation to food.

There was the crucial word – 'independent'. If we take it that the FSA is as good as its word, then we've got a neutral organisation here. However, all the FSA did was to commission the report, not write it. (But one could say that an independent organisation is not going to commission a study from a biased organisation.)

What about the London School of Hygiene and Tropical Medicine? They describe themselves here:

The London School of Hygiene and Tropical Medicine is Britain's national school of public health and a leading postgraduate institution worldwide for research and postgraduate education in global health.

There's nothing there to suggest anything but neutrality. Nor is there with regard to Dr Dangour.

The Soil Association, however, is (by its own admission) not a neutral organisation. It is very much pro-organic and against non-organic farming. This doesn't mean, of course, that its claims are not to be trusted. But it does mean that we would have to take its bias into account.

The European Union can be taken as neutral in this debate, being not obviously on one side or the other.

There's a lot of expertise about, so let's have a look at this criterion. Here's the London School of Hygiene and Tropical Medicine again:

> Part of the University of London, [it] is the largest institution of its kind in Europe with a remarkable depth and breadth of expertise encompassing many disciplines.

It's self-claimed expertise but it's unlikely that we're going to disagree. In addition, Dr Dangour's expertise is straightforwardly relevant. So what about the Soil Association? Their origins go back to 1946 and they have been concerned with developing organic standards since the 1970s. They clearly have expertise in this area, being able to provide expert advice to farmers and other groups.

With regard to reputation, we have nothing to worry about with any of these organisations. That of the London School is obviously considerable; the Soil Association provides the accepted standards for organic food.

So far, the criteria seem to have given a fairly evenly-matched contest (although the anti-organic case has so far scored a hit with regard to neutrality).

Let's bring in ability to perceive/sufficient access to see whether this separates the two sides. You will remember that Dr Dangour's team looked in all at 52,000 papers. This is an impressively large number. However, the Soil Association claims that Dr Dangour looked only at papers written in English, and did not take into account recent papers which showed the advantages of organic over non-organic food. This might limit the force of Dr Dangour's sufficient access but, in turn, we don't know whether the EU study took into account the papers studied by Dr Dangour and his team. So a bit of a cherry-picking draw there.

We're now into the area of motive. Is there any bias and/or vested interest? We'll have to acknowledge straight away that there is. The Soil Association's lack of neutrality on this issue has to be seen in terms of vested interest. If organic food was shown to have no health or nutritional advantages, then they would cease to have a justification for continuing to be active in promoting such food *in these terms*. However, there's no obvious vested interest on the other side (unless you can think of some!).

So it looks as if the Soil Association has lost on points...However, the Soil Association comes in with a late challenge. They point out that the FSA's restriction of the terms of reference to just looking at food (understandably, of course) ignores the wider issues of the (possible) effects of pesticides on health. For example, they refer to EU research that showed links between pesticides and certain cancers, male infertility, and nervous system disorders. They also refer to claimed environmental advantages of organic farming (although there is disagreement on these). In addition, there are higher animal welfare standards with organic farming...

So looking at the credibility of evidence took us so far, and then we're still left puzzling. Like custard, the claims started to run through our fingers even though we tried to hold them down. Who won this debate? You decide.

10

PRODUCING ARGUMENTS

Having got this far, we have seen how Critical Thinking, with the right approach, equips us with the skills of being able to understand and evaluate the claims and inferences in arguments.

But it should also do something else. It should equip us with the skill of being able to produce arguments. This is because, in an important way, we are doing the same thing. In producing (presumably, what we take to be good) arguments, we are looking at the significance of claims in order to see how inferences can be drawn from them.

So let's look at a list of things to do when putting together an argument.

- **Look carefully at the relationship between claims and inferences.** Ask yourself whether the claims (especially evidence-claims) are sufficient for the inference. What significance are you giving the claims? Could they have a different significance? Should the inference be reduced in scope to fit the claims better? Alternatively, do you need to add to the claims in order to increase the power of the reasons?

- **Be aware of the possible power of the counter-argument(s).** It can be a good idea to include this (them) and show how you can deal with such argument(s).

- **Look to draw inferences on the way to the main conclusion.** This can be useful in showing how your argument is built up, stage by stage. It's also useful for you to check that the lines of inference are working as they should.

- **Consider the role of evidence both in providing and in supporting the reasons.** Evidence can help in both of these ways. But you need to ask stern questions of your evidence. Is it of sufficient value to be able to use it in this way? Does it over-generalise? Are there *post hoc* issues with it? And so on. There's also the point about counter-examples. What force do they have? Not much, if they are merely examples of the occasional exception. But an example of yours might well be able to be stopped in its tracks by a counter-example.

- **Don't worry that your argument will be built on assumptions.** As we have seen, most arguments are. Those who say that a good argument should not contain assumptions are not competent Critical Thinkers. But, having said that, do be careful that the assumptions aren't necessary to bridge large shifts in the reasoning (as in slippery slope arguments).

- **Make sure that the argument fits together in a clear and coherent way.** The argument should proceed in steps that all contribute to the argument. An argument can gain strength by being well organised. This is partly as a result of the thinking you will have done in organising it: you'll have thought about sequences of reasoning; you'll have weighed up how the claims fit together; you'll have used evidence in the appropriate places. But the strength also comes from how clearly the argument will read. It won't distract the reader from the sequence of the case you're arguing. You'll take them by the hand and show them, bit by bit, what you want them to accept.

- **Make sure that the argument is consistent.** This is in some ways an aspect of coherence, but it's also a reminder that the claims and inferences in the argument should go in the same direction.

- **If you use analogies, think carefully about whether the similarities outweigh the differences.** Analogies are a way of making a point with some force. But only if the analogy has sufficient similarities. Here's one from Sir Martin Rees, President of the Royal Society (amongst other things). It's in an article in which he's arguing that everyone should have an understanding of science. 'You can appreciate the essence of science without being a scientist in the same way that you can appreciate music without being able to read a score or play an instrument.' What do you think? 'In the same way': is it?

- **Using hypothetical reasoning can give strength to an argument.** It allows you to explore lines of reasoning, without having to fully justify them. It allows you to fly kites to see how and where they might go. But do remember that hypothetical reasoning can support no more than hypothetical inferences.

● **Apply the standards that you would use to evaluate other arguments to your own.** Would you allow that evidence to be used like that? Would you allow that line of inference to go unquestioned? Would you stress that a different conclusion should have been drawn?

So that's it. You can do all these things. You can analyse and evaluate the lines of inference that are out there, in all their varieties (from the oddities of certain newspapers' online contributors to the arguments of the Astronomer Royal). You can also produce arguments which would meet the standards of the Critical Thinker.

So now you can reflect and comment on this item on the BBC website of 4 June 2009:

A sole can live cheerfully at a depth of 35,000 ft (10,933 m).

And this:

Americans are giving up their landlines at the rate of 700,000 per month. If this continues, the last cord will be cut in 2025. (*The Economist*, 13 August 2009)

Good thinking...

RESOURCES FOR FURTHER STUDY

Critical Thinking for AS Level (How To Books) This covers *everything* that you will need if you are taking the British OCR AS Level examination. But, despite its title, it also provides a thorough introduction to the skills involved in Critical Thinking for those of you who want to use them in any course of study. There are lots of examples and exercises.

Advanced Critical Thinking Skills (How To Books) This takes the skills introduced in the present book and extends and builds upon them. As a result, it will be especially useful for students on advanced level courses, whether this be in schools, colleges, or universities.

For those of you who just want to relax with family and friends for a Critical Thinking evening, then there's even a game of cards. It's called 'infer' (for obvious reasons), and it can be ordered from **www.ifthen.co.uk**

ADDITIONAL INFORMATION FOR THE EXERCISES

EXPLAINING AN EVIDENCE CLAIM (p.19)

You might have asked a number of questions about the evidence. Here are some which would be relevant.

- How is the word 'entrepreneur' defined?

- Is the definition of 'entrepreneur' the same in the US as it is in the UK?

- Is the definition of 'dyslexia' the same in the US as it is in the UK?

- Are the figures of 35 and 20 per cent significant?

- More specifically, what figure would we expect if the percentage of dyslexic entrepreneurs was the same as the percentage of the population that is dyslexic?

- If the figure is not the same (or not even nearly the same), what might be an (or the) explanation?

Though the percentage of people with dyslexia can vary depending on how different oprganisations estimate it, it is never as high as the 20 or 35 per cent given for entrepreneurs with dyslexia. The figure is likely to be around 10 per cent at the most.

The research that produced the evidence is described in the article 'Tracing Business Acumen to Dyslexia'. It can be found on *The New York Times* website at **http://www.nytimes.com/2007/12/06/business/06dyslexia.html?_r=2&ei=5087&em=&oref=slogin**

This gives suggested explanations, although doesn't give much information on the definition of 'entrepreneur' beyond the US figures being based on a study of '139 business owners in a wide range of fields across the United States'.

The explanations given are the following:

- Dyslexics were more than twice as likely as non-dyslexics to delegate authority.

- Dyslexics excel in oral communication.

- Dyslexics excel in problem-solving.

- Strategies that dyslexics have used since childhood to offset their weaknesses in written communication include being able to identify trustworthy people to whom responsibility can be delegated for taking major decisions.

- The difference between the US and the UK percentages is explained by 'earlier and more effective intervention by American schools to help dyslexic students deal with their learning problems.'

Inferences from these explanations could include the following:

- The UK should have a better strategy for helping dyslexics in schools.

- People with dyslexia should be recruited to work in organisations where the ability to delegate is important.

- People with dyslexia should be recruited to work in organisations where problem-solving abilities are important.

Hopefully, you'll have been able to see that asking explanatory questions about a simple evidence-claim can take you in all sorts of useful directions.

FINDING ASSUMPTIONS (p.38)

There are many assumptions being made here. Here's one:

- Injuries to students are a bad thing.

This might be so obvious as to not be worth mentioning but you can see that the author has to believe this to be true in order to draw their conclusion! (Try the negative test.)

Here are some others:

- The number of injuries from students doing gymnastics can be reduced.

- Improving the training of PE teachers can reduce the risk of injuries from gymnastics with their students.

- Students doing gymnastics will do what their teachers tell them.

- PE teachers will put their improved training into practice when teaching students gymnastics.

- Gymnastics is taught by PE teachers.

Here are some claims that are not assumed:

- Gymnastics has the highest rate of injuries for students.

- The number of students doing gymnastics is increasing.

- PE teachers do not know that gymnastics can cause injuries.

INDEX